Oramos Cantando
We Pray in Song

Cantos y Salmos para / Songs and Psalms
las Comunidades   for Latino/Anglo
Anglo-Latinas   Communities

Oramos Cantando
We Pray in Song

Cantos y Salmos para / **Songs and Psalms**
las Comunidades **for Latino/Anglo**
Anglo-Latinas **Communities**

Preview of
A Multicultural Hymnal for
Latino/Anglo Communities

Prevista de
Un Himnario Multicultural para
las Comunidades Anglo-Latinas

Singers Edition for Assembly and Choir
Edición para los Cantores: Asamblea y Coro

GIA Publications, Inc.
Chicago

Cover art by Rich Cruz.
Portada por Rich Cruz.

ISBN 1-57999-542-x

2 3 4 5 6 7 8 9 10 11 12 13 14 15 16 17 18 19 20

PREFACE

Toward the end of 2002 GIA Publications began work on a new, hardbound hymnal intended especially for multicultural, bilingual (Anglo/Latino) parishes. Far more than merely compiling a collection of music in two different languages, our mission has been to create a complete hymnal for the Latino community and a complete hymnal for the Anglo community under one cover, with virtually everything printed in both Spanish and English.

We have already completed work on the first complete bilingual version of the lectionary psalms for the full three-year cycle of Sundays and feasts. A sampling of seasonal psalms is included in this collection. They can be sung in either language alone, or bilingually.

While our core planning committee has already chosen the complete contents of the forthcoming hymnal, much translation work is still to be done. This small collection is a sampling of that work, and gives testimony to the extent to which our editors have reached out in gathering and commissioning outstanding texts. We have included hymns and songs for each season of the church year.

The finished hymnal — expected to be released near the end of 2006 — will contain more than 500 hymns and songs, including many of the fine Spanish language hymns published by OCP Publications. In the meantime, we offer this preview as a taste of that which is to come.

For bilingual and multicultural parishes throughout the United States, this book is not simply about the liturgical experience of today; it also opens the door to new possibilities. One such possibility — successfully experienced in places such as Taizé — is the simultaneous singing in multiple languages. For English-speakers and Spanish-speakers, that option can be found on every page of this collection.

GIA acknowledges Rev. Ronald F. Krisman, core committee chairman; core committee members María Dolores Martínez, PhD, Donna Peña, Rev. Juan J. Sosa; consultants Tony Alonso, Sr. Rosa María Icaza, CCVI, Rogelio Zelada; and GIA personnel Philip Roberts, (music engraving), Jeffry Mickus, (music engraving and book design), Michael Boschert (copyright clearances), Victoria Krstansky and Clarence Reiels (proofreaders), and Cathy Kennerk (administrative assistant).

Alec Harris
Publisher
Robert J. Batastini
Executive Editor

PREFACIO

Hacia el fin del año 2002 la casa editorial GIA comenzó a trabajar en un nuevo himnario encuadernado en pasta, destinado especialmente para las parroquias multiculturales y bilingües (anglo-latinas). Siendo mucho más que la simple recopilación de música en dos idiomas, nuestra misión ha sido crear un himnario completo para la comunidad latina y un himnario completo para la comunidad anglo en un solo volumen, con virtualmente todos los cantos impresos en español y en inglés.

Hemos terminado ya la preparación de la primera completa versión bilingüe de los salmos responsoriales del Leccionario para todos los domingos, las solemnidades, y las fiestas del Señor. Esta colección limitada presenta una muestra de los salmos estacionales que se encuentran en la obra completa. Se pueden entonar en un solo idioma, o en ambos.

Mientras que nuestro comité central de planificación ya ha seleccionado el contenido completo del próximo himnario, todavía falta mucho trabajo de traducción. Esta colección es un ejemplo de ese trabajo y testifica hasta que grado han llegado nuestros redactores para descubrir, seleccionar, y comisionar textos excepcionales. Hemos incluido aquí algunos himnos y canciones para cada estación del año litúrgico.

El himnario completo — que esperamos lanzar cerca del fin del 2006 — contendrá más de 500 himnos y cantos, incluyendo muchos de los hermosos himnos en español publicados por la casa editorial OCP. Mientras tanto, ofrecemos esta colección más pequeña para dar a probar lo que viene.

Para las parroquias bilingües y multiculturales en todos los Estados Unidos, este libro no se trata simplemente de la experiencia litúrgica de hoy; también abre la puerta a nuevas posibilidades. Una tal posibilidad – experimentada con éxito en lugares tal como Taizé en Francia – es el hecho de cantar simultáneamente en varios idiomas. Para los anglófonos y para los que hablan español, esta opción se encuentra en cada página de esta colección.

GIA quiere reconocer al comité central para el himnario completo – el encabezado, Rdo. Ronald F. Krisman, y los otros miembros, Dra. María Dolores Martínez, Donna Peña, y Rdo. Juan J. Sosa; también a los consultores: Tony Alonso, Hna. Rosa María Icaza, CCVI, Rogelio Zelada; y al personal de GIA: Philip Roberts, (grabador de música), Jeffry Mickus, (grabador de música y diseñador del libro), Michael Boschert (certificación de derechos de autor), Victoria Krstansky y Clarence Reiels (correctores de pruebas) y Cathy Kennerk (asistente administrativa).

Alec Harris
Editor
Robert J. Batastini
Editor Ejecutivo

Contents / Contenido

Hymns / Himnos

Indexes / Índices

1 Salmo 18: Señor, Tú Tienes Palabras
Psalm 19: Lord, You Have the Words

Respuesta, Bilingual Refrain / Respuesta Bilingüe

Se - ñor, Se - ñor, tú tie - nes pa - la - bras de
Lord, you have the words of ev - er -

vi - da e - ter - na. Se - ñor, tú tie - nes pa -
last - ing life. Se - ñor, tú tie - nes pa -

la - bras de vi - da e - ter - na.
la - bras de vi - da e - ter - na.

Refrain

Lord, you have the words of ev - er - last - ing life.

Lord, you have the words of ev - er - last - ing life.

Estrofas / Verses   Salmo 18 / Psalm 19:8, 9, 10, 11

1. La Ley del Señor es per - fecta y es descanso del alma;
2. Los mandatos del Se - ñor son rectos y alegran el co - ra - zón;
3. La voluntad del Se - ñor es pura y eternamen - te es - table;
4. Más precio - sos que el oro, más que el o - ro fino;

1. The law of the LORD is perfect, refreshing the soul;
2. The precepts of the LORD are right, rejoicing the heart;
3. The fear of the LORD is pure, enduring for - ever;
4. They are more pre - cious than gold, than a heap of pur - est gold;

1. el precepto del Se - ñor es fiel
2. la norma del Se - ñor es límpida
3. los mandamientos del Señor son ver - da - deros
4. más dulces que la miel

1. the decree of the LORD is trustworthy,
2. the command of the LORD is clear,
3. the ordinances of the LORD are true,
4. sweeter al - so than syrup

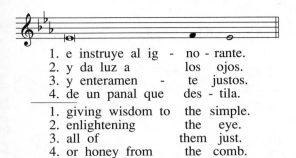

1. e instruye al ig - no - rante.
2. y da luz a los ojos.
3. y enteramen - te justos.
4. de un panal que des - tila.

1. giving wisdom to the simple.
2. enlightening the eye.
3. all of them just.
4. or honey from the comb.

Music: Repuesta / Refrain, Ronald F. Krisman; verses, Michel Guimont, © 1994, 1998, 2004, GIA Publications, Inc.

2 Salmo 21: Dios Mío, Dios Mío
Psalm 22: My God, My God

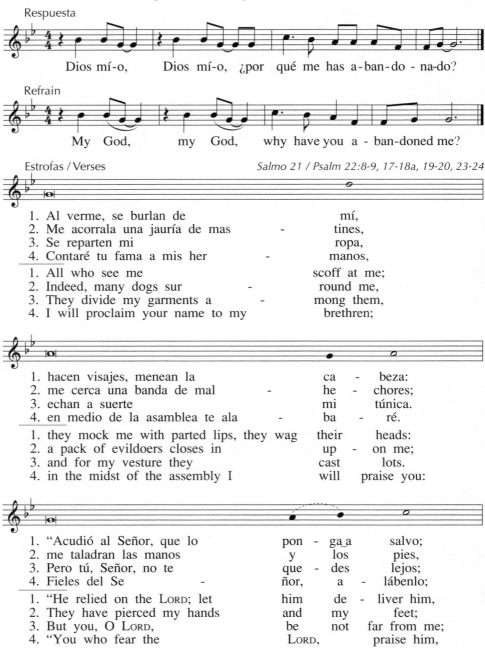

Respuesta

Dios mí-o, Dios mí-o, ¿por qué me has a-ban-do - na-do?

Refrain

My God, my God, why have you a - ban-doned me?

Estrofas / Verses   Salmo 21 / Psalm 22:8-9, 17-18a, 19-20, 23-24

1. Al verme, se burlan de   mí,
2. Me acorrala una jauría de mas   -   tines,
3. Se reparten mi   ropa,
4. Contaré tu fama a mis her   -   manos,

1. All who see me   scoff at me;
2. Indeed, many dogs sur   -   round me,
3. They divide my garments a   -   mong them,
4. I will proclaim your name to my   brethren;

1. hacen visajes, menean la   ca - beza:
2. me cerca una banda de mal   -   he - chores;
3. echan a suerte   mi   túnica.
4. en medio de la asamblea te ala   -   ba - ré.

1. they mock me with parted lips, they wag   their   heads:
2. a pack of evildoers closes in   up - on me;
3. and for my vesture they   cast   lots.
4. in the midst of the assembly I   will   praise you:

1. "Acudió al Señor, que lo   pon - ga a   salvo;
2. me taladran las manos   y   los   pies,
3. Pero tú, Señor, no te   que - des   lejos;
4. Fieles del Se   -   ñor,   a - lábenlo;

1. "He relied on the LORD; let   him   de - liver him,
2. They have pierced my hands   and   my   feet;
3. But you, O LORD,   be   not   far from me;
4. "You who fear the   LORD,   praise him,

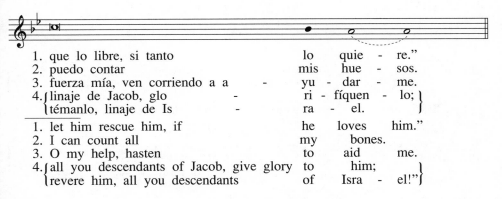

1. que lo libre, si tanto   lo   quie - re."
2. puedo contar   mis   hue - sos.
3. fuerza mía, ven corriendo a a   -   yu - dar - me.
4. {linaje de Jacob, glo   -   ri - fíquen - lo; }
   {témanlo, linaje de Is   -   ra - el. }

1. let him rescue him, if   he   loves   him."
2. I can count all   my   bones.
3. O my help, hasten   to   aid   me.
4. {all you descendants of Jacob, give glory to   him; }
   {revere him, all you descendants   of   Isra - el!"}

Music: Repuesta / Refrain, Tony E. Alonso; verses, Michel Guimont, © 1994, 1998, 2004, GIA Publications, Inc.

3 Salmo 22: El Señor Es Mi Pastor
Psalm 23: The Lord Is My Shepherd

Respuesta

El Se-ñor es mi pas-tor, na - da me fal - ta.

El Se-ñor es mi pas-tor, na - da me fal - ta.

Refrain

The Lord is my shep-herd; there is noth-ing I shall

want. The Lord is my shep-herd; noth-ing shall I fear.

Combined Refrains / Respuestas Combinadas

El Se-ñor es mi pas-tor, na - da me

fal - ta. El Se-ñor es mi pas-tor, na - da me fal-ta.

want. The Lord is my shep - herd; noth-ing shall I fear.

Estrofas / Verses

Salmo 22 / Psalm 23:1-3a, 3b-4, 5, 6

1. El Señor es mi pastor, na - da me falta:
2. Me guía por el sen - de - ro justo,
3. Preparas una me - sa an - te mí,
4. Tu bondad y tu misericordia me a - com - pañan

1. The LORD is my shepherd; I shall not want.
2. He guides me in right paths
3. You spread the ta - ble be - fore me
4. Only goodness and kind - ness follow me

1. en verdes praderas me hace re - cos - tar;
2. por el honor de su nombre.
3. enfrente de mis e - ne - migos,
4. todos los días de mi vida,

1. In verdant pastures he gives me re - pose;
2. for his name's sake.
3. in the sight of my foes;
4. all the days of my life;

1. me conduce hacia fuen - tes tran - quilas
2. { Aunque camine por caña - das os - curas,
   { tu vara y tu ca - yado
3. me unges la cabeza con per - fume,
4. y habitaré en la casa del Se - ñor,

1. Beside restful wa - ters he leads me;
2. { Even though I walk in the dark valley
   { With your rod and your staff
3. You anoint my head with oil;
4. And I shall dwell in the house of the LORD

1. y repa - ra mis fuer - zas.
2. nada temo, porque tú vas con - mi - go: }
   [———————————————] me so - sie - gan. }
3. y mi co - pa re - bo - sa.
4. por a - ños sin térmi - no.

1. he refresh - es my soul.
2. I fear no evil; for you are at my side. }
   that give me cour - age. }
3. my cup o - ver - flows.
4. for years to come.

Music: Repuesta / Refrain, Ronald F. Krisman; verses, Michel Guimont, © 1994, 1998, 2004, GIA Publications, Inc.

Salmo 24: A Ti, Señor 4
Psalm 25: To You, O Lord

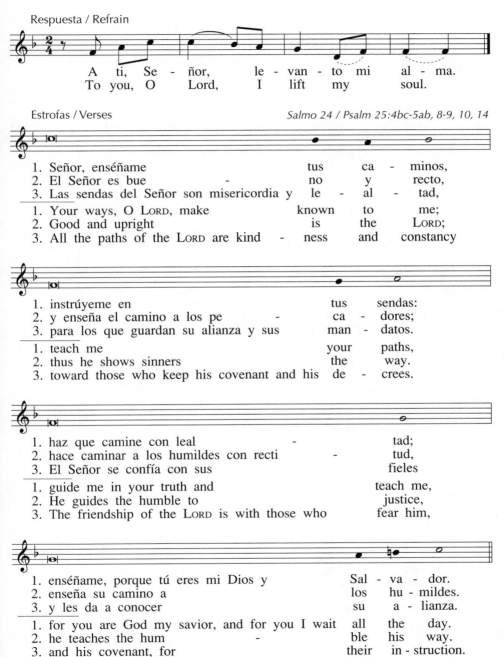

Respuesta / Refrain

A ti, Se - ñor, le - van - to mi al - ma.
To you, O Lord, I lift my soul.

Estrofas / Verses   *Salmo 24 / Psalm 25:4bc-5ab, 8-9, 10, 14*

1. Señor, enséñame   tus   ca - minos,
2. El Señor es bue -   no   y   recto,
3. Las sendas del Señor son misericordia y le - al - tad,

1. Your ways, O LORD, make   known to   me;
2. Good and upright   is   the LORD;
3. All the paths of the LORD are kind - ness and constancy

1. instrúyeme en   tus   sendas:
2. y enseña el camino a los pe - ca - dores;
3. para los que guardan su alianza y sus man - datos.

1. teach me   your   paths,
2. thus he shows sinners   the   way.
3. toward those who keep his covenant and his de - crees.

1. haz que camine con leal -   tad;
2. hace caminar a los humildes con recti - tud,
3. El Señor se confía con sus   fieles

1. guide me in your truth and   teach me,
2. He guides the humble to   justice,
3. The friendship of the LORD is with those who fear him,

1. enséñame, porque tú eres mi Dios y   Sal - va - dor.
2. enseña su camino a   los hu - mildes.
3. y les da a conocer   su   a - lianza.

1. for you are God my savior, and for you I wait all the day.
2. he teaches the hum -   ble his way.
3. and his covenant, for   their in - struction.

Music: Repuesta / Refrain, John Schiavone; verses, Michel Guimont, © 1994, 1998, 2004, GIA Publications, Inc.

5 Salmo 30: Padre, a Tus Manos
Psalm 31: Father, into Your Hands

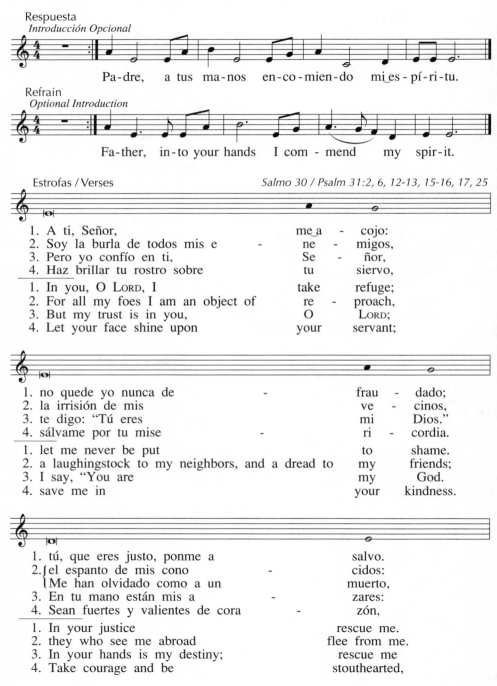

Respuesta
Introducción Opcional

Pa-dre, a tus ma-nos en-co-mien-do mi_es-pí-ri-tu.

Refrain
Optional Introduction

Fa-ther, in-to your hands I com - mend my spir-it.

Estrofas / Verses   Salmo 30 / Psalm 31:2, 6, 12-13, 15-16, 17, 25

1. A ti, Señor,   me_a - cojo:
2. Soy la burla de todos mis e   -   ne - migos,
3. Pero yo confío en ti,   Se - ñor,
4. Haz brillar tu rostro sobre   tu   siervo,

1. In you, O LORD, I   take   refuge;
2. For all my foes I am an object of   re - proach,
3. But my trust is in you,   O   LORD;
4. Let your face shine upon   your   servant;

1. no quede yo nunca de   -   frau - dado;
2. la irrisión de mis   ve - cinos,
3. te digo: "Tú eres   mi   Dios."
4. sálvame por tu mise   -   ri - cordia.

1. let me never be put   to   shame.
2. a laughingstock to my neighbors, and a dread to my friends;
3. I say, "You are   my   God.
4. save me in   your   kindness.

1. tú, que eres justo, ponme a   salvo.
2. {el espanto de mis cono   -   cidos:
   {Me han olvidado como a un   muerto,
3. En tu mano están mis a   -   zares:
4. Sean fuertes y valientes de cora   -   zón,

1. In your justice   rescue me.
2. they who see me abroad   flee from me.
3. In your hands is my destiny;   rescue me
4. Take courage and be   stouthearted,

1. {A tus manos encomien - do mi_es - píritu: }
   {tú, el Dios leal, me li - bra - rás. }
2. me ven por la calle, y esca - pan de mí. }
   me han desechado como a un cacha - rro in - útil. }
3. líbrame de los enemigos que me per - siguen.
4. los que esperan en el Se - ñor.

1. {Into your hands I com - mend my spirit; }
   {you will redeem me, O Lord, O faith - ful God. }
2. {I am forgotten like the unre - mem - bered dead; }
   {I am like a dish that is broken.}
3. from the clutches of my enemies and my persecutors."
4. all you who hope in the Lord.

Music: Repuesta / Refrain, Ronald F. Krisman; verses, Michel Guimont, © 1994, 1998, 2004, GIA Publications, Inc.

6 Salmo 50: Misericordia, Señor
Psalm 51: Be Merciful, O Lord

Respuesta / Refrain

Mi - se - ri - cor - dia, Se - ñor,
Be mer - ci - ful, O Lord,

he - mos pe - ca - do, he - mos pe - ca - do.
for we have sinned, for we have sinned.

Estrofas / Verses   *Salmo 50 / Psalm 51:3-4, 5-6, 12-13, 14, 17*

1. Misericordia, Dios mío, por tu   bon - dad,
2. Pues yo reconozco   mi   culpa,
3. Oh Dios, crea en mí un cora   -   zón   puro,
4. Devuélveme la alegría de tu sal   -   va - ción,

1. Have mercy on me, O God, in   your goodness;
2. For I acknowledge my   of - fense,
3. A clean heart create for me,   O   God,
4. Give me back the joy of your   sal - vation,

1. por tu inmensa compasión borra   mi   culpa;
2. tengo siempre presente mi   pe - cado:
3. renuévame por dentro con espíri   -   tu   firme;
4. afiánzame con espíritu ge   -   ne - roso.

1. in the greatness of your compassion wipe out my of - fense.
2. and my sin is before   me always:
3. and a steadfast spirit renew   with - in me.
4. and a willing spirit   sus - tain in me.

1. lava del todo mi   de - lito,
2. contra ti, contra ti solo   pe - qué,
3. no me arrojes lejos de   tu rostro,
4. Señor, me abrirás   los labios,

1. Thoroughly wash me from   my guilt
2. "Against you only have   I   sinned,
3. Cast me not out from   your presence,
4. O Lord, open   my lips,

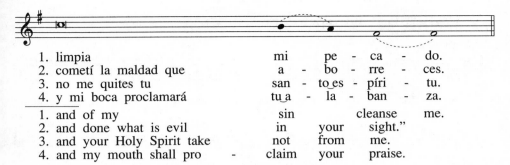

1. limpia   mi   pe - ca - do.
2. cometí la maldad que   a - bo - rre - ces.
3. no me quites tu   san - to_es - píri - tu.
4. y mi boca proclamará   tu_a - la - ban - za.

1. and of my   sin   cleanse me.
2. and done what is evil   in   your   sight."
3. and your Holy Spirit take   not   from   me.
4. and my mouth shall pro - claim   your   praise.

Music: Repuesta / Refrain, John Schiavone; verses, Michel Guimont, © 1994, 1998, 2004, GIA Publications, Inc.

7 Salmo 62: Mi Alma Está Sedienta
Psalm 63: My Soul Is Thirsting

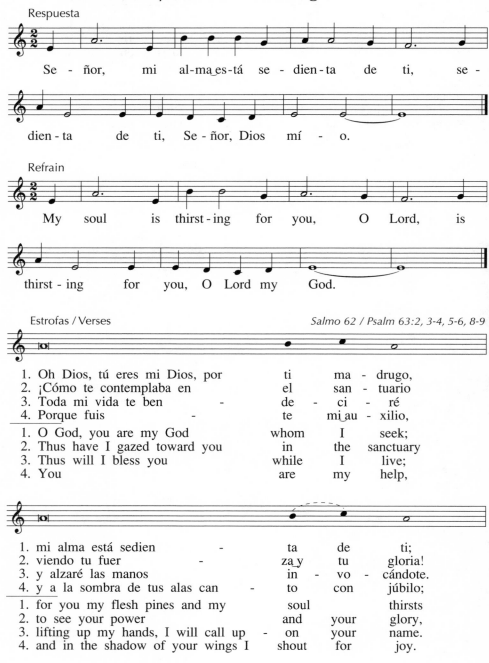

Respuesta

Se - ñor,   mi   al-ma es-tá   se - dien-ta   de   ti,   se -

dien-ta   de   ti,   Se - ñor,   Dios   mí - o.

Refrain

My   soul   is   thirst-ing   for   you,   O   Lord,   is

thirst-ing   for   you,   O   Lord   my   God.

Estrofas / Verses   *Salmo 62 / Psalm 63:2, 3-4, 5-6, 8-9*

1. Oh Dios, tú eres mi Dios, por   ti   ma - drugo,
2. ¡Cómo te contemplaba en   el   san - tuario
3. Toda mi vida te ben   -   de - ci - ré
4. Porque fuis   -   te   mi au - xilio,

1. O God, you are my God   whom   I   seek;
2. Thus have I gazed toward you   in   the   sanctuary
3. Thus will I bless you   while   I   live;
4. You   are   my   help,

1. mi alma está sedien   -   ta   de   ti;
2. viendo tu fuer   -   za y   tu   gloria!
3. y alzaré las manos   in - vo - cándote.
4. y a la sombra de tus alas can -   to   con   júbilo;

1. for you my flesh pines and my   soul   thirsts
2. to see your power   and   your   glory,
3. lifting up my hands, I will call up - on   your   name.
4. and in the shadow of your wings I shout for   joy.

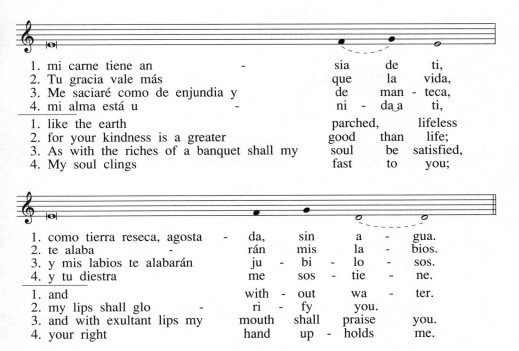

1. mi carne tiene an - sia de ti,
2. Tu gracia vale más que la vida,
3. Me saciaré como de enjundia y de man - teca,
4. mi alma está u - ni - da a ti,

1. like the earth parched, lifeless
2. for your kindness is a greater good than life;
3. As with the riches of a banquet shall my soul be satisfied,
4. My soul clings fast to you;

1. como tierra reseca, agosta - da, sin a - gua.
2. te alaba - rán mis la - bios.
3. y mis labios te alabarán ju - bi - lo - sos.
4. y tu diestra me sos - tie - ne.

1. and with - out wa - ter.
2. my lips shall glo - ri - fy you.
3. and with exultant lips my mouth shall praise you.
4. your right hand up - holds me.

Music: Repuesta / Refrain, Ronald F. Krisman; verses, Michel Guimont, © 1994, 1998, 2004, GIA Publications, Inc.

8 Salmo 65: Aclamen al Señor
Psalm 66: Let All the Earth

Respuesta

A - cla-men al Se - ñor, tie-rra_en-te - ra. A-

cla - men al Se - ñor, tie-rra_en-te - ra.

Refrain

Let all the earth cry out, cry out to God with joy.

Let all the earth cry out, cry out to God with joy.

Bilingual Refrains / Respuestas Bilingüe

Let all the earth cry out, cry out to God with joy. A-

cla - men al Se - ñor, tie-rra_en-te - ra.

Estrofas / Verses   *Salmo 65 / Psalm 66:1-3a, 4-5, 6-7a, 16, 20*

1. Aclamen al Se - ñor, tie - rra_en - tera;
2. Que se postre ante ti la tie - rra_en - tera,
3. Transformó el mar en tie - rra firme,
4. Fieles de Dios, vengan a_es - cu - char

1. Shout joyfully to God, all the earth,
2. Let all on earth worship and sing praise to you,
3. He has changed the sea in - to dry land;
4. Hear now, all you who fear God, while I de - clare

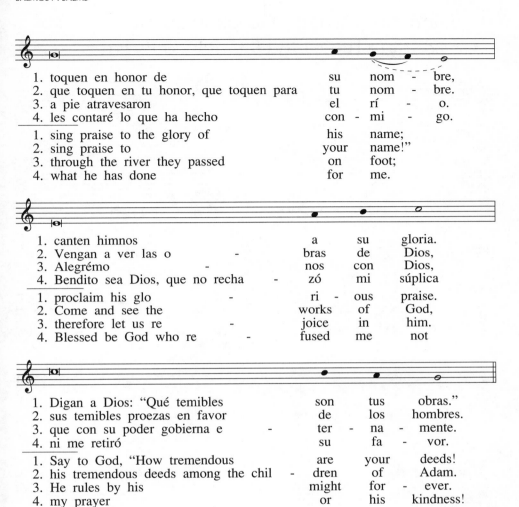

1. toquen en honor de su nom - bre,
2. que toquen en tu honor, que toquen para tu nom - bre.
3. a pie atravesaron el rí - o.
4. les contaré lo que ha hecho con - mi - go.

1. sing praise to the glory of his name;
2. sing praise to your name!"
3. through the river they passed on foot;
4. what he has done for me.

1. canten himnos a su gloria.
2. Vengan a ver las o - bras de Dios,
3. Alegrémo - nos con Dios,
4. Bendito sea Dios, que no recha - zó mi súplica

1. proclaim his glo - ri - ous praise.
2. Come and see the works of God,
3. therefore let us re - joice in him.
4. Blessed be God who re - fused me not

1. Digan a Dios: "Qué temibles son tus obras."
2. sus temibles proezas en favor de los hombres.
3. que con su poder gobierna e - ter - na - mente.
4. ni me retiró su fa - vor.

1. Say to God, "How tremendous are your deeds!
2. his tremendous deeds among the chil - dren of Adam.
3. He rules by his might for - ever.
4. my prayer or his kindness!

Music: Repuesta / Refrain, Ronald F. Krisman; verses, Michel Guimont, © 1994, 1998, 2004, GIA Publications, Inc.

9 Salmo 66: La Tierra Ha Dado Su Fruto
Psalm 67: The Earth Has Yielded Its Fruits

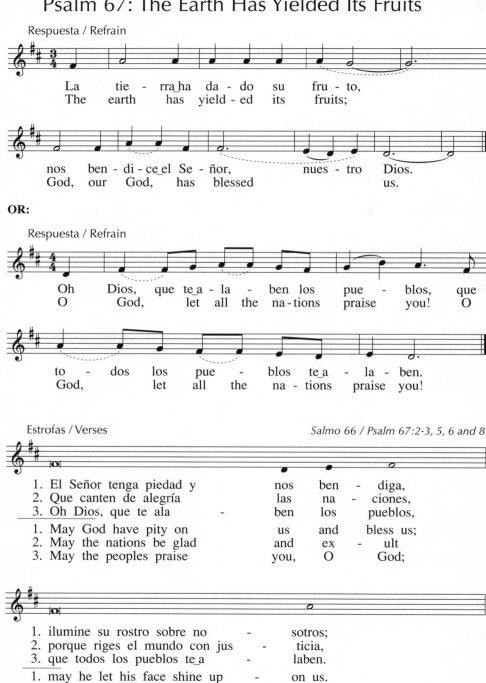

Respuesta / Refrain

La   tie - rra ha da - do su   fru - to,
The   earth has yield-ed its   fruits;

nos ben - di - ce el Se - ñor,   nues - tro Dios.
God, our God, has blessed   us.

OR:

Respuesta / Refrain

Oh   Dios, que te a - la - ben los pue - blos, que
O   God,   let all the na - tions praise you!   O

to - dos los pue - blos te a - la - ben.
God,   let all the na - tions praise you!

Estrofas / Verses   *Salmo 66 / Psalm 67:2-3, 5, 6 and 8*

1. El Señor tenga piedad y   nos ben - diga,
2. Que canten de alegría   las na - ciones,
3. Oh Dios, que te ala -   ben los pueblos,

1. May God have pity on   us   and bless us;
2. May the nations be glad   and ex - ult
3. May the peoples praise   you, O   God;

1. ilumine su rostro sobre no -   sotros;
2. porque riges el mundo con jus -   ticia,
3. que todos los pueblos te a -   laben.

1. may he let his face shine up -   on us.
2. because you rule the peoples in   equity;
3. may all the peoples   praise you!

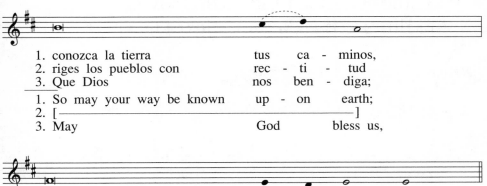

1. conozca la tierra   tus   ca - minos,
2. riges los pueblos con   rec - ti - tud
3. Que Dios   nos   ben - diga;

1. So may your way be known   up - on   earth;
2. [—————————————————]
3. May   God   bless us,

1. todos los pueblos tu   sal - va - ción.
2. y gobiernas las naciones   de   la   tie - rra.
3. que le teman hasta los confi - nes   del   or - be.

1. among all nations,   your   sal - va - tion.
2. the nations on the   earth you   guide.
3. and may all the ends of the   earth   fear   him!

Music: Repuesta / Refrain, Ronald F. Krisman, alternate Repuesta / Refrain, Tony E. Alonso; verses, Michel Guimont,
© 1994, 1998, 2004, GIA Publications, Inc.

10 Salmo 94: Ojalá Escuchen Hoy la Voz
Psalm 95: If Today You Hear His Voice

Respuesta*

O-ja-lá es-cu-chen hoy la voz del Se - ñor: "No en-du-rez-can el co - ra - zón." O-ja-lá es-cu-chen hoy la voz del Se - ñor: "No en-du-rez-can el co - ra - zón."

Refrain

If to-day you hear his voice, hard-en not your hearts.

If to-day you hear his voice, hard-en not your hearts.

Estrofas / Verses   *Salmo 94 / Psalm 95:1-2, 6-7, 8-9*

1. Vengan, aclamemos al Se - ñor,
2. Entren, postrémonos por tierra,
3. Ojalá escuchen hoy su voz:

1. Come, let us sing joyfully to the LORD;
2. Come, let us bow down in worship;
3. Oh, that today you would hear his voice:

1. demos vítores a la Roca que nos salva;
2. bendiciendo al Señor, creador nuestro.
3. "No endurezcan el corazón como en Meri - bá,

1. let us acclaim the Rock of our sal - vation.
2. let us kneel before the LORD who made us.
3. "Harden not your hearts as at Meribah,

For a bilingual refrain, sing the first half in one language, followed by the second half in the other.

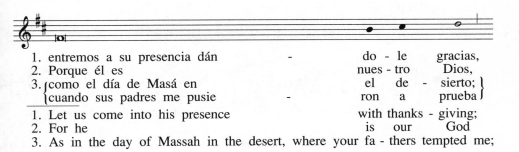

1. entremos a su presencia dán - do - le gracias,
2. Porque él es nues - tro Dios,
3. ⌠como el día de Masá en el de - sierto; ⌡
   ⌊cuando sus padres me pusie - ron a prueba⌡

1. Let us come into his presence with thanks - giving;
2. For he is our God
3. As in the day of Massah in the desert, where your fa - thers tempted me;

1. acla - mándo - lo con cantos.
2. y nosotros su pueblo, el rebaño que él guía.
3. y me ten - taron, aunque habían vis - to mis obras."

1. let us joyfully sing psalms to him.
2. and we are the people he shepherds, the flock he guides.
3. they tested me though they had seen my works."

Music: Repuesta / Refrain, Ronald F. Krisman; verses, Michel Guimont, © 1994, 1998, 2004, GIA Publications, Inc.

11   Salmo 97: Los Confines de la Tierra
Psalm 98: All the Ends of the Earth

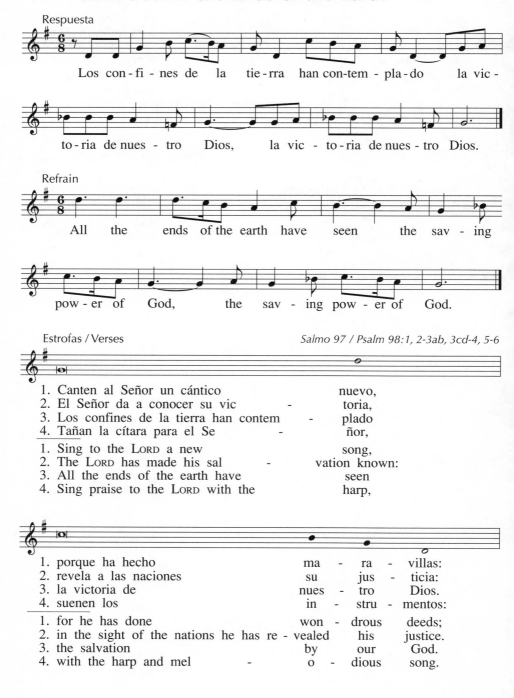

Respuesta

Los con-fi-nes de la tie-rra han con-tem - pla-do la vic -

to - ria de nues - tro Dios, la vic - to - ria de nues - tro Dios.

Refrain

All the ends of the earth have seen the sav - ing

pow - er of God, the sav - ing pow - er of God.

Estrofas / Verses   *Salmo 97 / Psalm 98:1, 2-3ab, 3cd-4, 5-6*

1. Canten al Señor un cántico   nuevo,
2. El Señor da a conocer su vic   -   toria,
3. Los confines de la tierra han contem   -   plado
4. Tañan la cítara para el Se   -   ñor,

1. Sing to the LORD a new   song,
2. The LORD has made his sal   -   vation known:
3. All the ends of the earth have   seen
4. Sing praise to the LORD with the   harp,

1. porque ha hecho   ma - ra - villas:
2. revela a las naciones   su   jus - ticia:
3. la victoria de   nues - tro Dios.
4. suenen los   in - stru - mentos:

1. for he has done   won - drous deeds;
2. in the sight of the nations he has re - vealed his justice.
3. the salvation   by our God.
4. with the harp and mel   -   o - dious song.

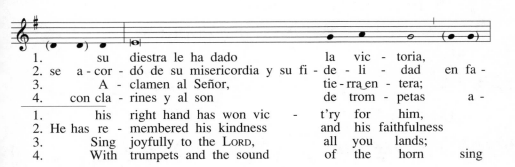

1.   su   diestra le ha dado   la   vic - toria,
2. se   a - cor - dó de su misericordia y su fi - de - li - dad   en fa -
3.   A - clamen al Señor,   tie - rra_en - tera;
4.   con cla - rines y al son   de trom - petas   a -

1.   his   right hand has won vic   - t'ry for   him,
2. He has re - membered his kindness   and his faithfulness
3.   Sing joyfully to the LORD,   all you   lands;
4.   With trumpets and the sound   of   the   horn   sing

1. su san   -   to   brazo.
2. vor de la casa de Is   - ra - el.
3. griten, vitore   -   en,   toquen.
4. clamen al Rey y   Se - ñor.

1. his ho   -   ly   arm.
2. toward the house   of Israel.
3. break into song;   sing praise.
4. joyfully before the King,   the   LORD.

Music: Repuesta / Refrain, Tony E. Alonso; verses, Michel Guimont, © 1994, 1998, 2004, GIA Publications, Inc.

12 Salmo 99: Somos Su Pueblo
Psalm 100: We Are His People

Respuesta

So - mos su pue - blo y_o - ve - jas de su re - ba - ño.

So - mos su pue - blo y_o - ve - jas de su re - ba - ño.

Refrain

We are his peo - ple, the sheep of his flock.

We are his peo - ple, the sheep of his flock.

Bilingual Refrain / Respuesta Bilingüe

So - mos su pue - blo y_o - ve - jas de su re - ba - ño.

We are his peo - ple, the sheep of his flock.

Estrofas / Verses

Salmo 99 / Psalm 100:1-2, 3, 5

1. Aclama al Señor,   tie - rra_en - tera,
2. Sepan que el Se -   ñor   es   Dios:
3. El Se -   ñor   es   bueno,

1. Sing joyfully to the LORD,   all   you   lands;
2. Know that the   LORD   is   God;
3. The   LORD   is   good:

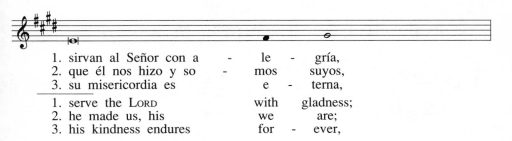

1. sirvan al Señor con a - le - gría,
2. que él nos hizo y so - mos suyos,
3. su misericordia es e - terna,

1. serve the LORD with gladness;
2. he made us, his we are;
3. his kindness endures for - ever,

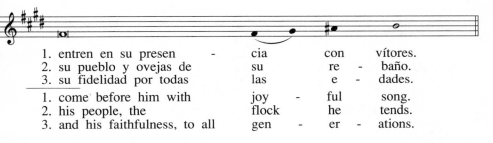

1. entren en su presen - cia con vítores.
2. su pueblo y ovejas de su re - baño.
3. su fidelidad por todas las e - dades.

1. come before him with joy - ful song.
2. his people, the flock he tends.
3. and his faithfulness, to all gen - er - ations.

Music: Repuesta / Refrain, Ronald F. Krisman; verses, Michel Guimont, © 1994, 1998, 2004, GIA Publications, Inc.

13 Salmo 103: Envía Tu Espíritu
Psalm 104: Lord, Send Out Your Spirit

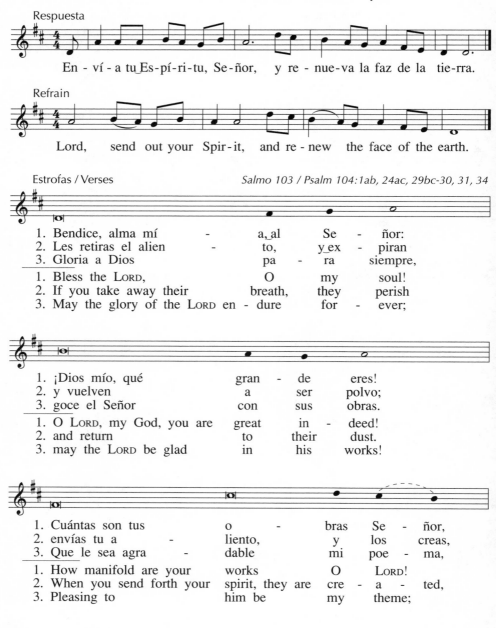

Respuesta

En - ví - a tu Es-pí-ri-tu, Se-ñor, y re - nue-va la faz de la tie-rra.

Refrain

Lord, send out your Spir-it, and re - new the face of the earth.

Estrofas / Verses   Salmo 103 / Psalm 104:1ab, 24ac, 29bc-30, 31, 34

1. Bendice, alma mí - a, al Se - ñor:
2. Les retiras el alien - to, y ex - piran
3. Gloria a Dios pa - ra siempre,

1. Bless the LORD, O my soul!
2. If you take away their breath, they perish
3. May the glory of the LORD en - dure for - ever;

1. ¡Dios mío, qué gran - de eres!
2. y vuelven a ser polvo;
3. goce el Señor con sus obras.

1. O LORD, my God, you are great in - deed!
2. and return to their dust.
3. may the LORD be glad in his works!

1. Cuántas son tus o - bras Se - ñor,
2. envías tu a - liento, y los creas,
3. Que le sea agra - dable mi poe - ma,

1. How manifold are your works O LORD!
2. When you send forth your spirit, they are cre - a - ted,
3. Pleasing to him be my theme;

1. la tierra está llena de   tus   cria - turas.
2. y repueblas la faz   de   la   tierra.
3. y yo me alegraré con   el   Se - ñor.

1. The earth is full   of   your   creatures.
2. and you renew the face   of   the   earth.
3. I will be glad   in   the   LORD.

Music: Repuesta / Refrain, Ronald F. Krisman; verses, Michel Guimont, © 1994, 1998, 2004, GIA Publications, Inc.

14 Salmo 115: El Cáliz Que Bendecimos
Psalm 116: Our Blessing-Cup

Respuesta

El cá - liz que ben-de - ci - mos es la co - mu - nión de la san - gre de Cris - to. El cá - liz que ben-de - ci - mos es la co - mu - nión de la san - gre de Cris - to.

Refrain

Our bless - ing - cup is a com - mun - ion with the Blood of Christ. Our bless - ing - cup is a com - mun - ion with the Blood of Christ.

Bilingual Refrain / Respuesta Bilingüe

Our bless - ing - cup is a com - mun - ion with the Blood of Christ. El cá - liz que ben-de - ci - mos es la co - mu - nión de la san - gre de Cris - to.

Estrofas / Verses   *Salmo 115 / Psalm 116:12-13, 15-16bc, 17-18*

1. ¿Como pagaré   al   Se - ñor
2. Mucho le cues   -   ta al   Se - ñor
3. Te ofreceré un sacrificio   de a - la - banza,

1. How shall I make a return   to   the   LORD
2. Precious in the eyes   of   the   LORD
3. To you will I offer sacrifice   of   thanks - giving,

1. todo el bien que   me ha   hecho?
2. la muerte de   sus   fieles.
3. invocando tu nombre,   Se -   ñor.

1. for all the good he has done   for   me?
2. is the death of   his   faithful ones.
3. and I will call upon the name of   the   LORD.

1. Alzaré la copa de la salva   -   ción,
2. Señor, yo soy tu siervo, hijo de tu es - clava:
3. Cumpliré al Señor mis   votos

1. The cup of salvation I will take   up,
2. I am your servant, the son of your   handmaid;
3. My vows to the LORD I will   pay

1. invocan   -   do   su   nombre.
2. rompiste   mis   ca -   denas.
3. en presencia de   to -   do el   pueblo.

1. and I will call upon the name   of   the   LORD.
2. you have   loosed my   bonds.
3. in the presence of   all   his   people.

Music: Repuesta / Refrain, Ronald F. Krisman; verses, Michel Guimont, © 1994, 1998, 2004, GIA Publications, Inc.

15 Salmo 117: Éste Es el Día
Psalm 118: This Is the Day

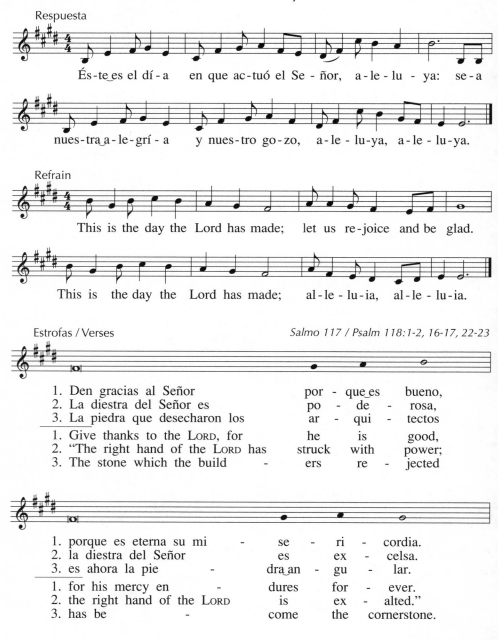

Respuesta

És-te_es el dí-a   en que ac-tuó el Se-ñor, a-le-lu-ya: se-a

nues-tra_a-le-grí-a   y nues-tro go-zo,   a-le-lu-ya, a-le-lu-ya.

Refrain

This is the day the Lord has made;   let us re-joice and be glad.

This is   the day the   Lord has made;   al-le-lu-ia,   al-le-lu-ia.

Estrofas / Verses   *Salmo 117 / Psalm 118:1-2, 16-17, 22-23*

1. Den gracias al Señor   por - que_es   bueno,
2. La diestra del Señor es   po - de - rosa,
3. La piedra que desecharon los   ar - qui - tectos

1. Give thanks to the LORD, for   he   is   good,
2. "The right hand of the LORD has   struck with   power;
3. The stone which the build -   ers   re - jected

1. porque es eterna su mi - se - ri - cordia.
2. la diestra del Señor   es   ex - celsa.
3. es ahora la pie - dra_an - gu - lar.

1. for his mercy en - dures   for - ever.
2. the right hand of the LORD   is   ex - alted."
3. has be - come   the   cornerstone.

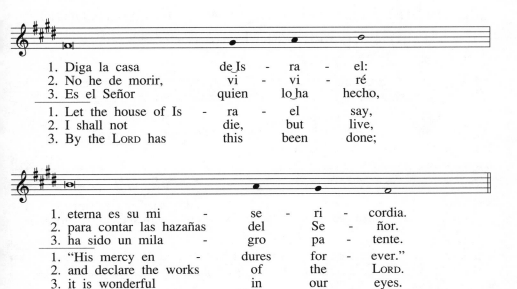

1. Diga la casa   de Is - ra - el:
2. No he de morir,   vi - vi - ré
3. Es el Señor   quien lo ha hecho,

1. Let the house of Is - ra - el say,
2. I shall not   die, but live,
3. By the LORD has   this been done;

1. eterna es su mi - se - ri - cordia.
2. para contar las hazañas del Se - ñor.
3. ha sido un mila - gro pa - tente.

1. "His mercy en - dures for - ever."
2. and declare the works of the LORD.
3. it is wonderful in our eyes.

Music: Repuesta / Refrain, Ronald F. Krisman; verses, Michel Guimont, © 1994, 1998, 2004, GIA Publications, Inc.

16   Salmo 129: Del Señor Viene la Misericordia
Psalm 130: With the Lord There Is Mercy

Respuesta / Refrain*

Del Se - ñor   vie - ne   la   mi - se - ri - cor - dia,   la
With the   Lord,   with the   Lord   there is   mer - cy,   and

re - den-ción co - pio - sa.   Del Se - ñor   vie - ne la mi - se - ri -
full - ness   of   re - demp-tion.   With the Lord,   with the Lord   there is

cor - dia,   la   re - den-ción   co -   pio - sa.
mer - cy,   and   full - ness of   re -   demp-tion.

Estrofas / Verses   *Salmo 129 / Psalm 130:1-2, 3-4ab, 4c-6, 7-8*

1. Desde lo hondo a ti grito, Se - ñor;
2. Si llevas cuentas de los delitos, Se - ñor,
3. Mi alma espera en el Se - ñor,
4. Porque del Señor viene la miseri - cordia,

1. Out of the depths I cry to you, O LORD;
2. If you, O LORD, mark in - iquities,
3. I trust in the LORD;
4. For with the LORD is kindness

1. Señor, escu - cha mi voz;
2. ¿quién podrá re - sis - tir?
3. espera en su pa - labra;
4. la reden - ción co - piosa;

1. LORD, hear my voice!
2. LORD, who can stand?
3. my soul trusts in his word.
4. and with him is plen - teous re - demption;

For a bilingual refrain, sing the first half in one language, followed by the second half in the other.

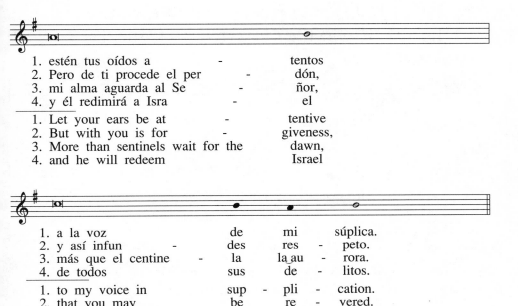

1. estén tus oídos a - tentos
2. Pero de ti procede el per - dón,
3. mi alma aguarda al Se - ñor,
4. y él redimirá a Isra - el

1. Let your ears be at - tentive
2. But with you is for - giveness,
3. More than sentinels wait for the dawn,
4. and he will redeem Israel

1. a la voz de mi súplica.
2. y así infun - des res - peto.
3. más que el centine - la la au - rora.
4. de todos sus de - litos.

1. to my voice in sup - pli - cation.
2. that you may be re - vered.
3. let Israel wait for the LORD.
4. from all their in - iquities.

Music: Repuesta / Refrain, Ronald F. Krisman; verses, Michel Guimont, © 1994, 1998, 2004, GIA Publications, Inc.

17 Lucas 1:46-55: El Poderoso Ha Hecho
Luke 1:46-55: The Almighty Has Done Great Things

Respuesta

El Po-de - ro - so_ha he - cho o - bras gran-des por mí,

el Po-de - ro - so_ha he - cho o - bras gran-des por mí:

su nom-bre_es san - to, su nom-bre_es san - to.

Refrain

The Al - might - y has done great things for me,

the Al - might - y has done great things for me and

ho - ly is his Name, ho - ly is his Name.

Bilingual Refrain / Respuesta Bilingüe

The Al - might - y has done great things for me,

el Po-de - ro - so_ha he - cho o - bras gran-des por mí: and

ho - ly is his Name, su nom-bre_es san - to.

Estrofas / Verses   *Lucas 1 / Luke 1:46-47, 48-49, 50-51, 52-53, 54-55*

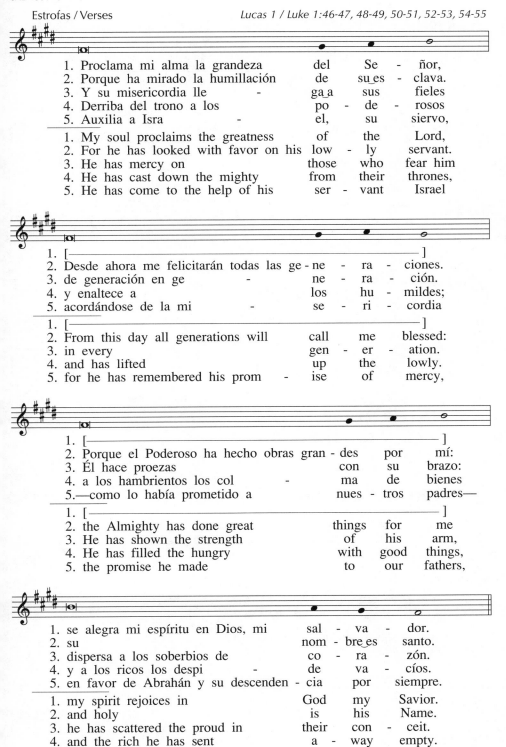

1. Proclama mi alma la grandeza   del   Se - ñor,
2. Porque ha mirado la humillación   de   su_es - clava.
3. Y su misericordia lle - ga_a sus fieles
4. Derriba del trono a los   po - de - rosos
5. Auxilia a Isra - el, su siervo,

1. My soul proclaims the greatness   of   the   Lord,
2. For he has looked with favor on his low - ly servant.
3. He has mercy on those who fear him
4. He has cast down the mighty from their thrones,
5. He has come to the help of his ser - vant Israel

1. [——————————————————————]
2. Desde ahora me felicitarán todas las ge - ne - ra - ciones.
3. de generación en ge - ne - ra - ción.
4. y enaltece a los hu - mildes;
5. acordándose de la mi - se - ri - cordia

1. [——————————————————————]
2. From this day all generations will call me blessed:
3. in every gen - er - ation.
4. and has lifted up the lowly.
5. for he has remembered his prom - ise of mercy,

1. [——————————————————————]
2. Porque el Poderoso ha hecho obras gran - des por mí:
3. Él hace proezas con su brazo:
4. a los hambrientos los col - ma de bienes
5.—como lo había prometido a nues - tros padres—

1. [——————————————————————]
2. the Almighty has done great things for me
3. He has shown the strength of his arm,
4. He has filled the hungry with good things,
5. the promise he made to our fathers,

1. se alegra mi espíritu en Dios, mi sal - va - dor.
2. su nom - bre_es santo.
3. dispersa a los soberbios de co - ra - zón.
4. y a los ricos los despi - de va - cíos.
5. en favor de Abrahán y su descenden - cia por siempre.

1. my spirit rejoices in God my Savior.
2. and holy is his Name.
3. he has scattered the proud in their con - ceit.
4. and the rich he has sent a - way empty.
5. to Abraham and his child - ren for ever.

Music: Repuesta / Refrain, Ronald F. Krisman; verses, Michel Guimont, © 1994, 1998, 2004, GIA Publications, Inc.

18 KYRIE

Se-ñor, ten pie-dad.

Cris-to, ten pie-dad. Se-ñor, ten pie-dad.

Ky-ri-e e-le-i-son. Chri-ste e-le-i-son.

Ky-ri-e e-le-i-son. Lord, have mer-cy.

Christ, have mer-cy. Lord, have mer-cy.

*All or sections of (A), (B), and (C) may be used as desired.

Music: Donna Peña; acc. by Tony E. Alonso, © 2005, GIA Publications, Inc.

19 GOSPEL ACCLAMATION / ACLAMACIÓN ANTES DEL EVANGELIO

Refrain / Estribillo

Glo-ry and praise to you, Lord Je-sus Christ.
Glo-ria y_ho-nor a ti, Se-ñor Je-sús.

Glo-ry and praise to
Glo-ria y_ho-nor a

Music: Donna Peña; acc. by Tony E. Alonso, © 2005, GIA Publications, Inc.

20 SANCTUS / SANTO

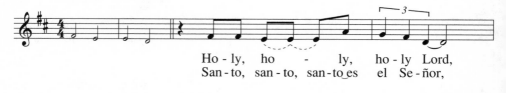

Ho - ly, ho - ly, ho - ly Lord,
San - to, san - to, san - to es el Se - ñor,

God of pow - er and   might,   heav - en and earth are
Dios del u - ni - ver - so.   Lle - nos es - tán   el

full of your glo - ry.   Ho - san - na in the   high - est.
cie - lo y la tie - rra,   lle - nos de tu   glo - ria.

Ho - san - na in the   high - est.   Bless - ed is he who
Ho - san - na en el   cie - lo.   Ben - di - to   el que

comes in   the name of the Lord. Ho - san - na in the high - est.
vie - ne en nom - bre del Se - ñor. Ho - san - na en el cie - lo.

MEMORIAL ACCLAMATION   21

Christ has died, Christ is ris-en, Christ will come a - gain. Christ has died, Christ is ris-en, Christ will come a - gain.

Text: ICEL, © 1973
Music: Donna Peña; acc. by Tony E. Alonso, © 2005, GIA Publications, Inc.

ACLAMACIÓN AL MEMORIAL   22

Cri - sto ha muer - to. Cri - sto ha re - su - ci - ta - do. Cris - to ven - drá, ven - drá de nue - vo.

Music: Donna Peña; acc. by Tony E. Alonso, © 2005, GIA Publications, Inc.

23 AMEN / AMÉN

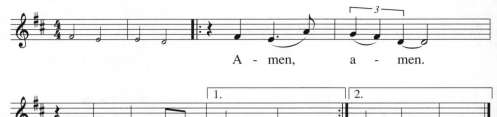

A - men, a - men.

A - men, a - men.

1.

2.

men.

Music: Donna Peña; acc. by Tony E. Alonso, © 2005, GIA Publications, Inc.

24 LAMB OF GOD

Lamb of   God,   you

take a - way   the   sins of   the world: have

mer - cy   on   us.   Lamb of   God,   you

take   a - way   the   sins of   the world:

grant   us   peace,   grant   us peace.

Music: Donna Peña; acc. by Tony E. Alonso, © 2005, GIA Publications, Inc.

CORDERO DE DIOS

Cor - de-ro de Dios, que

qui-tas el pe - ca-do del mun - do, ten pie -

dad de no - so-tros. Cor - de-ro de Dios, que

qui-tas el pe - ca-do del mun - do,

da - nos la paz, da - nos la paz.

Music: Donna Peña; acc. by Tony E. Alonso, © 2005, GIA Publications, Inc.

26 O Come, O Come, Emmanuel
Oh Ven, Oh Ven, Emanuel

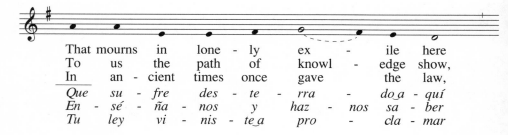

1. O   come,   O   come,   Em - man - u - el,
2. O   come,   O   Wis - dom   from   on   high,
3. O   come,   O   come,   great   Lord   of   might,

1. Oh   ven,   oh   ven,   E - ma - nu - el,
2. Sa - bi - du - rí - a   ce - les - tial,
3. Oh   ven,   oh   ven,   oh   A - do - nai,

And   ran - som   cap - tive   Is - ra - el,
Who   or - ders   all   things   might - i - ly;
Who   to   your   tribes   on   Si - nai's   height

Li - bra_al   cau - ti - vo   Is - ra - el,
Al   mun - do   hoy   ven   a   mo - rar.
Que_en tiem - po_a - trás   en   Si - na - í,

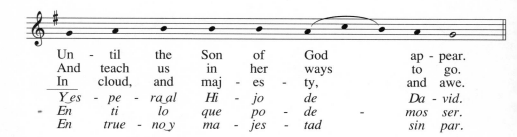

That mourns   in   lone - ly   ex - ile   here
To   us   the   path   of   knowl - edge   show,
In   an - cient   times   once   gave   the   law,

Que   su - fre   des - te - rra - do_a - quí
En - sé - ña - nos   y   haz - nos   sa - ber
Tu   ley   vi - nis - te_a   pro - cla - mar

Un - til   the   Son   of   God   ap - pear.
And   teach   us   in   her   ways   to   go.
In   cloud,   and   maj - es - ty,   and   awe.

Y_es - pe - ra_al   Hi - jo   de   Da - vid.
En   ti   lo   que   po - de - mos   ser.
En   true - no_y   ma - jes - tad   sin   par.

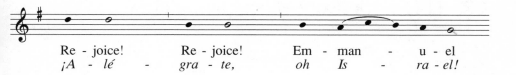

Re - joice! Re - joice! Em - man - u - el
¡A - lé - gra - te, oh Is - ra - el!

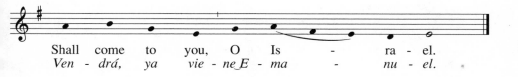

Shall come to you, O Is - ra - el.
Ven - drá, ya vie - ne E - ma - nu - el.

4. O come, O Rod of Jesse's stem,
   From ev'ry foe deliver them
   That trust your mighty power to save,
   And give them vict'ry o'er the grave.

5. O come, O Key of David, come,
   And open wide our heav'nly home;
   Make safe the way that leads on high,
   And close the path to misery.

6. O come, O Dayspring from on high
   And cheer us by your drawing nigh;
   Disperse the gloomy clouds of night,
   And death's dark shadow put to flight.

7. O come, Desire of nations, bind
   In one the hearts of humankind;
   O bid our sad divisions cease,
   And be for us our King of Peace.

4. *Oh ven, tú, Vara de Isaí,*
   Redime al pueblo infeliz
   Del poderío infernal,
   Y dale vida celestial.

5. *Oh ven, tú, Llave de David,*
   Abre el celeste hogar feliz;
   Haz que lleguemos bien allá,
   Y cierra el paso a la maldad.

6. *Oh ven, Aurora Matinal,*
   Y con tu adviento sin igual,
   Disipa toda oscuridad,
   Y alúmbrenos tu claridad.

7. *Anhelo de los pueblos, ven;*
   En ti podremos paz tener;
   De crueles guerras líbranos,
   Y reine soberano, Dios.

Text: *Veni, veni Emmanuel*; Latin 9th C.; English tr. by John M. Neale, 1818-1866, alt.; Spanish tr. vss. 1, 4, 5, Alfred Ostrom, 1868-1941, © 1964,
   Publicaciones *El Escudo;* vss. 2, 7, Federico J. Pagura, b.1923, © 1962; vss. 3, 6, Dimas Planas-Belfort, 1934-1992, © Editorial Avance Luterano
Tune: VENI VENI EMMANUEL, LM with refrain; Mode I; adapt. by Thomas Helmore, 1811-1890; acc. by Richard Proulx, b.1937, © 1975,
   GIA Publications, Inc.

27 El Dios de Paz / Peace-giving God

Estrofas / Verses

1. El Dios de paz, el Ver - bo e - ter - no,
2. Vie - ne a en - se - ñar - nos el sen - de - ro,
3. Por u - na sen - da o s - cu - re - ci - da
1. Peace - giv - ing God and Word e - ter - nal,
2. You come to teach sal - va - tion's path - way,
3. All those who walk in gloom and shad - ows,

En nues - tras al - mas va a mo - rar.
Vie - ne a tra - er - nos el per - dón.
Va - mos en bus - ca de la luz.
Come dwell with - in each long - ing soul.
Guid - ing with mer - cy all the lost.
Seek here a new and glo - rious Light.

Él es la Luz, Ca - mi - no y Vi - da,
Vie - ne a mo - rir en un ma - de - ro,
Luz y a - le - grí - a sin me - di - da
You are the Light that shines in dark - ness;
You came to die at Cal - v'ry's cross - road,
Light of a - bun - dant joy and glad - ness,

Gra - cia y per - dón pa - ra el mor - tal.
Pre - cio de nues - tra re - den - ción.
En - con - tra - re - mos en Je - sús.
Yours is the grace that makes us whole.
Pay - ing for us the dead - ly cost.
We shall be - hold in Je - sus Christ.

Estribillo / Refrain

Ven,   Sal - va - dor,   ven   sin   tar - dar;
Come   quick -ly,   Lord;   Come with - out   de - lay.

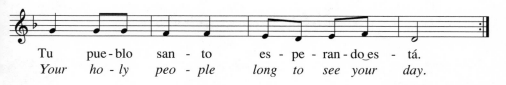

Tu   pue - blo   san - to   es - pe - ran - do_es - tá.
Your   ho - ly   peo - ple   long   to   see   your   day.

4. Brilla_en la noche nueva_Aurora,
   Sol de justicia, Sol de paz.
   Toda la_humanidad añora
   Al que la viene a salvar.

5. Nuestro Señor vendrá un día,
   Lleno de gracia_y majestad,
   Para llevar al pueblo suyo
   Hacia su reino celestial.

4. *Bring to our night your radiant dawning,*
   Christ, Sun of Righteousness and Peace.
   Nations and peoples seek your justice,
   Crying with prayers that never cease:

5. *Lord, come at last in flesh to save us,*
   Filled with majestic grace and love,
   Leading and lifting all your children
   Up to your joyous courts above!

Texto: Anónimo; adapt. por el comité editorial del himnario *Albricias*; tr. por Mary Louise Bringle, n.1953, © 2005, GIA Publications, Inc.
Música: EL DIOS DE PAZ, 9 8 9 8 con estribillo; Melodía hebrea; arm. por Ronald F. Krisman, n.1946, © 2005, GIA Publications, Inc.

28 My Soul in Stillness Waits
En el Silencio Te Aguardo

Refrain / Estribillo

For you, O Lord, my soul in still-ness waits,
En el si - len - cio te_a-guar-do_a ti, Se - ñor.

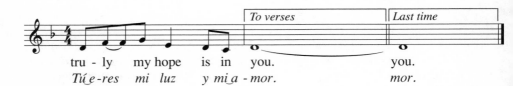

To verses / Last time

tru - ly my hope is in you. you.
Tú_e -res mi luz y mi_a - mor. mor.

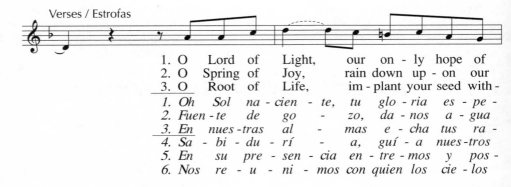

Verses / Estrofas

1. O Lord of Light, our on - ly hope of
2. O Spring of Joy, rain down up - on our
3. O Root of Life, im - plant your seed with -
1. *Oh Sol na - cien - te, tu glo - ria es - pe -*
2. *Fuen -te de go - zo, da - nos a - gua*
3. *En nues -tras al - mas e - cha tus ra -*
4. *Sa - bi - du - rí - a, guí - a nues -tros*
5. *En su pre - sen - cia en - tre - mos y pos -*
6. *Nos re - u - ni - mos con quien los cie - los*

glo - ry, Your ra - diance shines in all who look to
spir - its, Our thirst - y hearts are yearn - ing for your
in us, And in your ad - vent, draw us all to
ra - mos Y tu bri - llar en nues - tro co - ra
vi - va. Ver - bo de Dios, te - ne - mos sed de
í - ces. Por tu lle - ga - da_a - trá - e - nos a
pa - sos. Aun -que bus - ca - mos, no_hay sa - tis - fac-
tré - mo-nos. El co - ra - zón a - bra - mos al Se -
hi - zo, De las mon - ta - ñas y ma - res, el Crea-

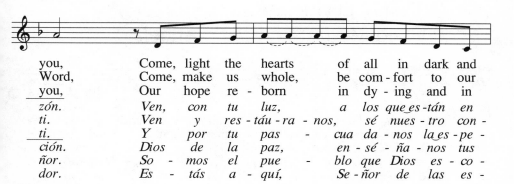

you,	Come,	light	the	hearts	of	all	in	dark and
Word,	Come,	make	us	whole,	be	com - fort	to	our
you,	Our	hope	re - born		in	dy - ing	and	in
zón.	_Ven,_	_con_	_tu_	_luz,_	_a_	_los que_es -tán_	_en_	
_ti._	_Ven_	_y_	_res - táu - ra - nos,_		_sé_	_nues - tro_	_con -_	
_ti._	_Y_	_por_	_tu_	_pas_ -	_cua_	_da - nos la_es - pe -_		
ción.	_Dios_	_de_	_la_	_paz,_	_en - sé - ña - nos_	_tus_		
ñor.	_So - mos_	_el_	_pue_ -		_blo que Dios_	_es - co -_		
dor.	_Es - tás_	_a - quí,_			_Se -ñor_	_de_	_las_	_es -_

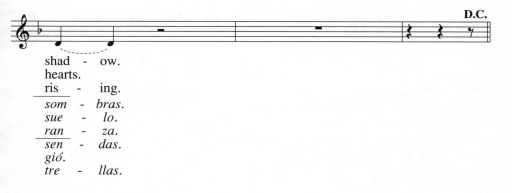

D.C.

| shad - ow. |
| hearts. |
| ris - ing. |
| _som - bras._ |
| _sue - lo._ |
| _ran - za._ |
| _sen - das._ |
| _gió._ |
| _tre - llas._ |

4. O Key of Knowledge, guide us in our pilgrimage,
   we ever seek, yet unfulfilled remain,
   open to us the pathway of your peace.

5. Come, let us bow before the God who made us,
   let ev'ry heart be opened to the Lord,
   for we are all the people of his hand.

6. Here we shall meet the Maker of the heavens,
   Creator of the mountains and the seas,
   Lord of the stars, and present to us now.

Text: Psalm 95 and "O" Antiphons; Marty Haugen, b.1950; tr. by Ronald F. Krisman, b.1946
Tune: Marty Haugen, b.1950
© 1982, 2005, GIA Publications, Inc.

29 O Come, Divine Messiah!
¡Divino Mesías! El Mundo Anhela

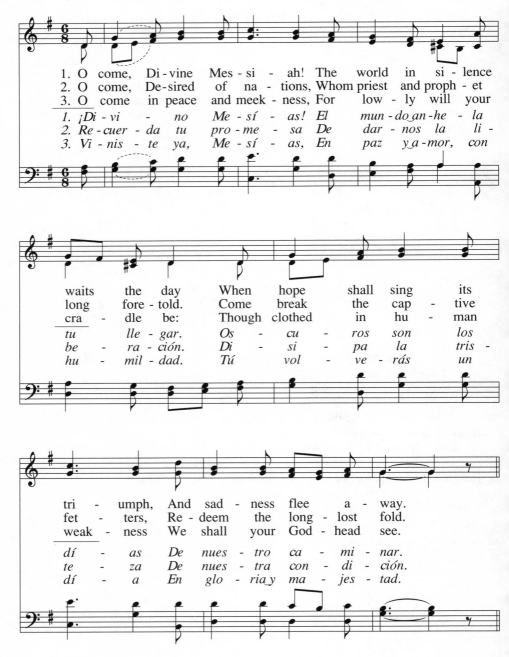

1. O come, Di-vine Mes-si - ah! The world in si - lence
2. O come, De-sired of na - tions, Whom priest and proph - et
3. O come in peace and meek - ness, For low - ly will your

1. ¡Di - vi - no Me - sí - as! El mun - do_an-he - la
2. Re - cuer - da tu pro - me - sa De dar - nos la li -
3. Vi - nis - te ya, Me - sí - as, En paz y_a-mor, con

waits the day When hope shall sing its
long fore - told. Come break the cap - tive
cra - dle be: Though clothed in hu - man

tu lle - gar. Os - cu - ros son los
be - ra - ción. Di - si - pa la tris -
hu - mil - dad. Tú vol - ve - rás un

tri - umph, And sad - ness flee a - way.
fet - ters, Re - deem the long - lost fold.
weak - ness We shall your God - head see.

dí - as De nues - tro ca - mi - nar.
te - za De nues - tra con - di - ción.
dí - a En glo - ria_y ma - jes - tad.

Dear Sav - ior, haste! Come, come to earth. Dis - pel the
¡Ven, Sal - va - dor! Da - nos tu_a - mor. Que - re - mos

night and show your face, And bid us hail the dawn of
con - tem - plar tu faz. ¡So - có - rre - nos, no tar - des

grace. O come, Di - vine Mes - si - ah! The
más! ¡Di - vi - no Me - sí - as, Ven

world in si - lence waits the day When hope shall sing its
pron - to, nues - tro Re - den - tor! Que bri - llen nues - tros

tri - umph, And sad - ness flee a - way.
dí - as Por tu ve - nir, Se - ñor.

Text: *Venez, divin Messie;* Abbé Simon-Joseph Pellegrin, 1663-1745; English tr. by Sr. Mary of St. Philip, 1825-1904, alt.; Spanish tr. by
    Ronald F. Krisman, b.1946, © 2005, GIA Publications, Inc.
Tune: VENEZ, DIVIN MESSIE, 7 8 7 6 with refrain; French Noël, 16th C.; harm by Healey Willan, 1880-1968, © 1958, The Basilian Fathers,
    assigned to Ralph Jusko Publications, Inc.

30 Hacia Belén / On the Road to David's City

Estrofas / Verses

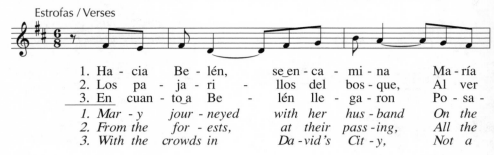

1. Ha - cia Be - lén, se_en - ca - mi - na Ma - rí - a
2. Los pa - ja - ri - llos del bos - que, Al ver
3. En cuan - to_a Be - lén lle - ga - ron Po - sa -

1. Mar - y jour - neyed with her hus - band On the
2. From the for - ests, at their pass - ing, All the
3. With the crowds in Da - vid's Cit - y, Not a

con su_a - man - te_es - po - so, Lle - van - do_en su com - pa -
pa - sar los es - po - sos, Les can - ta - ban me - lo -
da_al pun - to pi - die - ron, Na - die les qui - so_hos - pe -

road to Da - vid's Cit - y. She was bear - ing Christ our
birds came swift - ly wing - ing As they watched this lov - ing
sin - gle inn was a - ble To give shel - ter to the

ñí - a A to - do_un Dios po - de - ro - so.
dí - as Con sus tri - nos ar - mo - nio - sos.
dar Por - que tan po - bres les vie - ron.

Sav - ior, On - ly Son of God Al - might - y.
cou - ple, And burst in - to hap - py sing - ing.
cou - ple, But a poor and low - ly sta - ble.

Estribillo / Refrain

A - le - grí - a,_a - le - grí - a,_a - le - grí - a, A - le -
A - le - grí, a - le - grí, a - le - grí - a! O what

grí - a,_a - le - grí - a_y pla - cer, Que la
joy and what glad - ness were there When the

Vir - gen va de pa - so Con su_es -
Vir - gin and her hus - band Made their

1.
po - so_ha - cia Be - lén.
way to Da -vid's Cit -y.

2.
Last time
po - so_ha - cia Be - lén.
way to Beth -le - hem.

Texto: Anónimo; tr. por Mary Louise Bringle, n.1953, © 2005, GIA Publications, Inc.
Musica: Tradicional de Puerto Rico; arm. por Ronald F. Krisman, n.1946, © 2005, GIA Publications, Inc.

31 Silent Night, Holy Night / Noche de Paz

1. Si - lent night, ho - ly night, All is calm,
2. Si - lent night, ho - ly night, Shep - herds quake
3. Si - lent night, ho - ly night, Son of God,

1. No - che de paz, no - che de a - mor. To - do duer - me en
2. No - che de paz, no - che de a - mor. O - ye hu - mil - de el
3. No - che de paz, no - che de a - mor. Mi - ra qué gran

all is bright Round yon Vir - gin
at the sight; Glo - ries stream from
love's pure light Ra - diant beams from

de - rre - dor, En - tre los as - tros que es -
fiel pas - tor, Co - ros ce - les - tes que a -
res - plan - dor Lu - ce en el ros - tro del

Moth - er and Child, Ho - ly In - fant so
heav - en a - far, Heav'n - ly hosts sing
thy ho - ly face, With the dawn of re -

par - cen su luz, Be - lla, a - nun - cian - do al ni -
nun - cian sa - lud, Gra - cias y glo - rias en
ni - ño Je - sús, En el pe - se - bre, del

ten - der and mild,   Sleep   in   heav - en - ly
al - le - lu - ia;   Christ,   the   Sav - ior, is
deem - ing grace,   Je - sus,   Lord,   at thy
ñi - to Je - sús,   Bri - lla la es - tre - lla de
gran ple - ni - tud,   Por nues - tro   buen   Re - den -
mun - do la luz,   As - tro de e - ter - no ful -

peace,   Sleep   in   heav - en - ly   peace.
born!   Christ,   the   Sav - ior, is   born!
birth,   Je - sus,   Lord,   at thy   birth.
paz,   Bri - lla la es - tre - lla de   paz.
tor,   Por nues - tro   buen   Re - den - tor.
gor,   As - tro de e - ter - no ful - gor.

Text: *Stille Nacht, heilige Nacht;* Joseph Mohr, 1792-1848; English tr. by John F. Young, 1820-1885; Spanish tr. by Federico Fliedner, 1845-1901
Tune: STILLE NACHT, 66 89 66; Franz X. Gruber, 1787-1863

32 Ha Nacido el Niño Dios / Il Est Né
He Is Born! Now the Child Has Come!

Estribillo / Refrain

(Español) ¡Ha na - ci - do el ni - ño Dios, To - quen las
(Français) Il est né, le di - vin En - fant, Jou - ez, haut -
(English) He is born! Now the child has come! Fill all the

flau - tas y los tam - bo - res! ¡Ha na - ci - do el ni - ño
bois, ré - son - nez, mu - set - tes! Il est né, le di - vin En -
air with our mer - ry car - ol - ling! Play the pipe, beat the joy - ful

Dios, A - la - be - mos al Sal - va - dor!
fant; Chan - tons tous son a - vè - ne - ment!
drum! Hope is born, for the child has come!

Estrofas / Verses

1. La pro - fé - ti - ca a - nun - cia - ción Del Me -
2. ¡Oh, cuán be - llas es la tier - na faz De es - te
3. El Cre - a - dor de to - do ser, Co - mo

1. Faith - ful sag - es through a - ges long, Proph - ets
2. See what light from his face has shone, Grace and
3. Je - sus, Sov'r - eign and Ho - ly One, We a -

sí - as que es - pe - ra el pue - blo Se ha cum - pli - do con
ni - ño que tra - jo el cie - lo! Su her - mo - sa hu -
ni - ño vie - ne a no - so - tros. Al Cre - a - dor de

sang of the Sav - ior's com - ing: Faith - ful sag - es through
mer - cy of God re - veal - ing; See what light from his
dore you, be - fore you kneel - ing; Je - sus, Sov'r - eign and

D.C.

pre - ci - sión:	¡Ha lle - ga - do la sal - va - ción!
ma - ni - dad	Es re - ga - lo de e - ter - ni - dad.
to - do ser	A - la - bé - mos - le al na - cer.
a - ges long,	*Proph - ets sang of the prom - ised dawn.*
face has shone,	*From this child, from the prom - ised one!*
Ho - ly One,	*Dwell in us, make our hearts your throne!*

Text: French carol, 19th C.; English tr. by Andrew Donaldson, b.1951, © 1997; Spanish tr. by Jorge Alfonso Lockward, © 1996, Abingdon Press
Tune: IL EST NÉ, 8 10 8 8 with refrain; French carol, 18th C.; harm. by Carlton R. Young, b.1926, © 1989, The United Methodist Publishing House

33 Joy to the World / Al Mundo Paz

1. Joy to the world! the Lord is come: Let earth re-
2. Joy to the world! the Sav - ior reigns: Let us, our
3. He rules the world with truth and grace, And makes the

1. ¡Al mun - do paz, na - ció Je - sús, Na - ció ya
2. ¡Al mun - do paz, el Sal - va - dor En tie - rra
3. ¡Al mun - do Dios go - ber - na - rá Con gra - cia y

[⌢]

ceive her King; Let ev - 'ry heart pre-
songs em - ploy; While fields and floods, rocks,
na - tions prove The glo - ries of his

nues - tro Rey! El co - ra - zón ya
rei - na - rá! Ya es fe - liz el
con po - der! A las na - cio - nes

pare him room, And heav'n and na - ture
hills, and plains Re - peat the sound - ing
right - eous - ness, And won - ders of his

tie - ne luz, Y paz su san - ta
pe - ca - dor, Je - sús per - dón le
mos - tra - rá Su_a - mor y su po -

And
Re -
And

Y
Je -
Su_a -

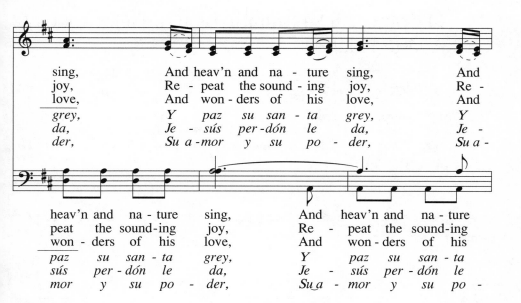

sing,	And heav'n and na - ture sing,	And
joy,	Re - peat the sound - ing joy,	Re -
love,	And won - ders of his love,	And
grey,	Y paz su san - ta grey,	Y
da,	Je - sús per -dón le da,	Je -
der,	Su a -mor y su po - der,	Su a -

heav'n and na - ture	sing,	And	heav'n and na - ture
peat the sound-ing	joy,	Re -	peat the sound-ing
won - ders of his	love,	And	won - ders of his
paz su san - ta	grey,	Y	paz su san - ta
sús per - dón le	da,	Je -	sús per - dón le
mor y su po -	der,	Su a -	mor y su po -

heav'n,	and	heav'n	and	na - ture	sing.
peat,	re -	peat	the	sound - ing	joy.
won -	ders,	won -	ders	of his	love.
paz,	y	paz	su	san - ta	grey.
sús,	Je -	sús	per - dón	le	da.
mor,	su a -	mor	y	su po -	der.

sing,	and	heav'n	and	na - ture	sing.
joy,	re -	peat	the	sound - ing	joy.
love,	and	won -	ders	of his	love.
grey,	y	paz	su	san - ta	grey.
da,	Je -	sús	per - dón	le	da.
der,	su a -	mor	y	su po -	der.

Text: Psalm 98; Isaac Watts, 1674-1748; tr. anonymous
Tune: ANTIOCH, CM with repeat; arr. from George F. Handel, 1685-1759, in T. Hawkes' *Collection of Tunes*, 1833

34 O Come, All Ye Faithful / Venid, Fieles Todos / Adéste Fidéles

1. O come, all ye faith-ful, joy-ful and tri-um-phant, O
2. ⸭ God of God, Light of Light,
1. Ve - nid, fie - les to - dos, a Be - lén mar - che - mos De
2. El que_es Hi -jo_e - ter - no del e - ter-no Pa - dre, Y
1. Ad - é - ste fi - dé - les, laé - ti, tri - um -phán - tes, Ve -
2. ⸭ De - um de De - o, Lu - men de Lú - mi-ne

come ye, O come ye to Beth - le - hem;
Lo! He comes forth from the Vir - gin's womb.
go - zo triun - fan - tes, y lle - nos de_a-mor; Y_al
Dios ver - da - de - ro que_al mun - do cre - ó, Al
ní - te, ve - ní - te in Béth - le - hem.
Ge - stant pu - él - lae ví - sce - ra.

Come and be - hold him, born the King of an - gels;
Our ver - y God, be - got - ten not cre - a - ted,
Rey de los cie - los con - tem -plar po - dre - mos;
se - no vir - gí - neo vi - no de_u - na ma - dre;
Na - tum vi - dé - te, Re - gem an - ge - ló - rum.
De - um ve - rum, Gé - ni - tum, non fa - ctum.

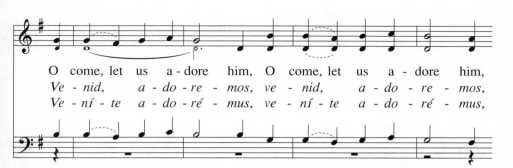

O come, let us a-dore him, O come, let us a-dore him,
Ve - nid, a - do - re - mos, ve - nid, a - do - re - mos,
Ve - ní - te a - do - ré - mus, ve - ní - te a - do - ré - mus,

O come, let us a - dore him, Christ, the Lord!
ve - nid, a - do - re - mos a Cris - to_el Se - ñor.
ve - ní - te a - do - ré - mus Dó - mi - num.

3. Sing, choirs of angels,
   sing in exultation,
   Sing, all ye citizens of heav'n above!
   Glory to God, all
   glory in the highest;

3. *Cantad jubilosas,*
   célicas criaturas:
   Resuenen los cielos con vuestra canción;
   ¡Al Dios bondadoso,
   gloria en las alturas;

4. Yea, Lord, we greet thee,
   born this happy morning,
   Jesus, to thee be all glory giv'n;
   Word of the Father,
   now in flesh appearing;

4. *Jesús, celebramos*
   tu bendito nombre
   Con himnos solemnes de grato loor;
   Por siglos eternos
   todo ser te adore;

3. *Cantet nuncio,*
   chorus angelorum,
   Cantet nunc aula caeléstium.
   Glória, glória, in excélsis Deo.

4. *Ergo qui natus*
   Die hodiérna,
   Jesu tibi sit glória.
   Patris aeternae verbum caro factum.

Text: *Adeste fideles;* John F. Wade, c.1711-1786; English tr. by Frederick Oakeley, 1802-1880, alt.; Spanish tr. by Juan Bautista Cabrera, 1837-1916
Tune: ADESTE FIDELES, Irregular with refrain; John F. Wade, c.1711-1786

35 Star-Child / Niño: Es Astro

Last time to Coda ⊕

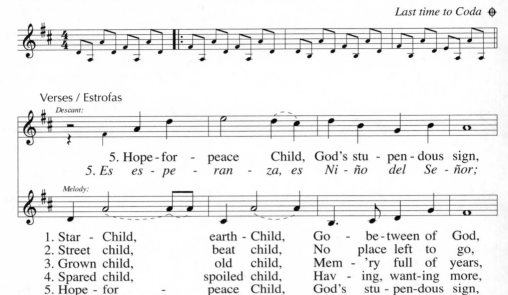

Verses / Estrofas

Descant:

5. Hope-for - peace Child, God's stu - pen-dous sign,
5. *Es es - pe - ran - za, es Ni - ño del Se - ñor;*

Melody:

1. Star - Child,	earth - Child,	Go - be - tween of God,
2. Street child,	beat child,	No place left to go,
3. Grown child,	old child,	Mem - 'ry full of years,
4. Spared child,	spoiled child,	Hav - ing, want-ing more,
5. Hope - for peace Child,	God's stu - pen-dous sign,
1. *Ni - ño: es as - tro,*	*Me - dia - dor de Dios;*
2. *Ni - ño a - bu - sa - do,*	*Po - bre y sin ho - gar;*
3. *Ni - ño: ha cre - ci - do;*	*¡Cuán - to ha de a - ño - rar!*
4. *Ni - ño e - xi - gen - te,*	*Tie - ne y quie - re más;*
5. *Es es - pe - ran - za, es Ni - ño del Se - ñor;*

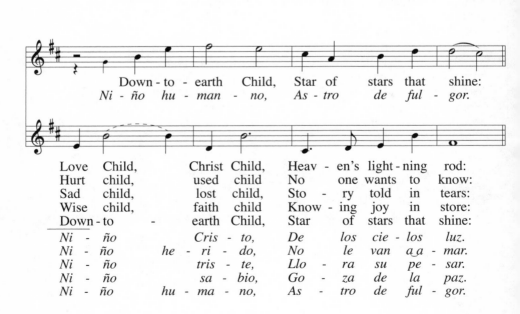

Down - to - earth Child, Star of stars that shine:
Ni - ño hu - man - no, As - tro de ful - gor.

Love Child,	Christ Child,	Heav - en's light - ning rod:
Hurt child,	used child	No one wants to know:
Sad child,	lost child,	Sto - ry told in tears:
Wise child,	faith child	Know - ing joy in store:
Down - to earth Child,	Star of stars that shine:
Ni - ño Cris - to,	*De los cie - los luz.*
Ni - ño he - ri - do,	*No le van a a - mar.*
Ni - ño tris - te,	*Llo - ra su pe - sar.*
Ni - ño sa - bio,	*Go - za de la paz.*
Ni - ño hu - ma - no,	*As - tro de ful - gor.*

Refrain / Estribillo

This year,   this   year   let the   day ar -
Oh   Dios,   da - le   en   es - ta   Na - vi -

This year,   this   year   let   the day ar -
Oh   Dios,   da - le   en   es - ta   Na - vi -

rive   When   Christ - mas comes for   ev - 'ry - one,
dad   Un   dí - a   de   fe - li - ci - dad

rive   When   Christ - mas comes for   ev - 'ry - one,
dad   Un   dí - a   de   fe - li - ci - dad

⊕ Coda

ev - 'ry - one   a - live.
a   la hu - ma - ni - dad.

ev - 'ry - one   a - live.
a   la hu - ma - ni - dad.

Text: Shirley Erena Murray, b.1931, ©1994, Hope Publishing Co.; tr. by Raquel Gutíerrez-Achón and George Lockwood, © 1997, Hope Publishing Co.
Tune: NOAH'S SONG, 4 5 4 5 with refrain; Ronald F. Krisman, b.1946, © 2003, GIA Publications, Inc.

36 Go Tell It on the Mountain
Ve, Grita en la Montaña

Refrain / Estribillo

Go tell it on the moun - tain, O - ver the hills and
Ve, gri - ta en la mon - ta - ña, so - bre los mon - tes

ev - 'ry - where; Go tell it on the
por do - quier; Ve, gri - ta en la mon-

moun - tain That Je - sus Christ is born!
ta - ña Que Cris - to ya na - ció.

Verses / Estrofas

1. While shep - herds kept their watch - ing O'er
2. The shep - herds feared and trem - bled When
3. Down in a low - ly man - ger The
1. *Pas - to - res, sus re - ba - ños De*
2. *Y lue - go, a - som - bra - dos, O -*
3. *En un pe - se - bre hu - mil - de El*

si - lent flocks by night, Be - hold through - out the
lo! a - bove the earth Rang out the an - gel
hum - ble Christ was born, And God sent us sal -
no - che al cui - dar, Con gran sor - pre - sa
ye - ron el can - tar De án - ge - les en
Cris - to ya na - ció. De Dios a - mor su-

D.C.

heav - ens	There	shone	a	ho - ly	light.
cho - rus	That	hailed	our	Sav - ior's	birth.
va - tion	That	bless - ed		Christ - mas	morn.
vie - ron	*Glo -*	*rio - sa*		*luz*	*bri - llar.*
co - ro	*Las*	*nue - vas*		*pro - cla -*	*mar.*
bli - me	*Al*	*mun - do*		*des - cen -*	*dió.*

Text: African-American spiritual; adapt. by John W. Work, Jr., 1871-1925, © Mrs. John W. Work, III; tr. by Anita González, alt., ©
Tune: GO TELL IT ON THE MOUNTAIN, 7 6 7 6 with refrain; African-American spiritual; harm. by Robert J. Batastini, b.1942, © 1995, GIA
    Publications, Inc.

37 What Child Is This / ¿Qué Niño Es Éste?

1. What child is this, who, laid to rest, On
2. Why lies he in such mean es - tate Where
3. So bring him in - cense, gold and myrrh, Come

1. ¿Qué ni - ño_es és - te que_al dor - mir En
2. ¿Por qué_en hu - mil - de_es - ta - blo_a - sí El
3. Trai - ga - mos do - nes en su_ho - nor, Oh

Mar - y's lap is sleep - ing? Whom an - gels greet with
ox and ass are feed - ing? Good Chris - tian, fear; for
peas - ant, king to own him; The King of kings sal -

bra - zos de Ma - rí - a, Pas - to - res ve - lan,
ni - ño ha na - ci - do? Por to - do_in -jus - to
pue - blos y na - cio - nes, Al Rey de re - yes,

an - thems sweet, While shep - herds watch are keep - ing?
sin - ners here The si - lent Word is plead - ing.
va - tion brings, Let lov - ing hearts en - throne him.

án - ge - les Le can - tan me - lo - dí - as?
pe - ca - dor Su_a - mor ha flo - re - ci - do.
Sal - va - dor, Un tro - no le - van - te - mos.

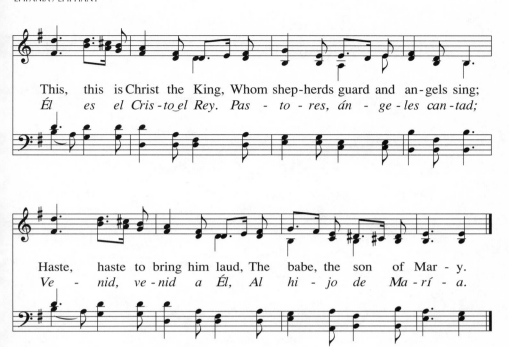

This,   this is Christ the King, Whom shep-herds guard and an-gels sing;
Él   *es*   *el Cris-to el Rey. Pas* - *to - res, án* - *ge - les can-tad;*

Haste,   haste to bring him laud, The   babe, the son   of Mar - y.
Ve - *nid, ve - nid a Él, Al   hi - jo de   Ma - rí - a.*

Text: William C. Dix, 1837-1898; tr. by Angel M. Mergal, 1909-1971
Tune: GREENSLEEVES, 8 7 8 7 with refrain; English melody, 16th C.; harm. by John Stainer, 1840-1901

38 Perdona a Tu Pueblo, Señor
Forgive Us, Your People

Estribillo / Refrain

Per - do - na_a tu pue - blo, Se - ñor, per - do - na_a tu
For -give   us, your peo - ple, O Lord.   For - give   us, your

To repeat refrain

pue - blo, per - dó - na - le, Se - ñor.
peo - ple, for - give us, ho - ly Lord.

| 1.-7. | *To verses* | 8. |

ñor.   ñor.
Lord.   *Lord.*

Estrofas / Verses

1. No_es - tés   e - ter - na - men - te_e - no - ja -
2. Por   las   pro - fun - das   lla -   gas cru - e -
3. Por   las   he - ri - das   de   pies y   ma -
1. Look   not   up - on   your   peo - ple with wrath, O
2. You   stretch your arms   to   love   and to   heal, O
3. For   wounds that   we   in - flict   on your hands, O

do,   No_es - tés e - ter - na - men - te_e - no -
les,   Por   las   sa - li - vas   y   por las
nos,   Por   los   a - zo - tes   tan   in - hu -
Christ.   *Look   not up - on your peo - ple with*
Christ.   *We   an - swer love with hate; now we*
Christ,   *For   hurt and vio - lence spread through our*

D.S.

ja - do:	Per - dó - na - le,	Se - ñor.
hie - les:	Per - dó - na - le,	Se - ñor.
ma - nos:	Per - dó - na - le,	Se - ñor.
wrath, O Christ:	*For - give us,*	*ho - ly Lord.*
kneel, O Christ:	*For - give us,*	*ho - ly Lord.*
lands, O Christ:	*For - give us,*	*ho - ly Lord.*

4. Por los tres clavos que te clavaron,
   Y las espinas que te punzaron:
   Perdónale, Señor.

5. Por las tres horas de tu agonía,
   En que por Madre diste a María:
   Perdónale, Señor.

6. Por la abertura de tu costado,
   No estés eternamente enojado:
   Perdónale, Señor.

7. Por ese amor que nos redimía
   Y es nuestra fuerza de cada día:
   Perdónale, Señor.

4. *For dignity we mock with our thorns,*
   O Christ;
   For outcast ones we jeer at and scorn,
   O Christ: Forgive us, holy Lord.

5. *For hours you spent in pain on the cross,*
   O Christ;
   With Mary, comfort all stunned by loss,
   O Christ: Forgive us, holy Lord.

6. *For all the sorrows borne on your path,*
   O Christ;
   Look not upon your people with wrath,
   O Christ: Forgive us, holy Lord.

7. *With love that draws us back when*
   we stray, O Christ,
   Redeeming us afresh every day,
   O Christ: Forgive us, holy Lord.

Texto: Anónimo; tr. por Mary Louise Bringle, n.1953, © 2005, GIA Publications, Inc.
Música: Anónimo; arm. por Ronald F. Krisman, n.1946, © 2005, GIA Publications, Inc.

39 Return to God / Volvamos Hoy a Nuestro Dios

Refrain / Estribillo

Re - turn to God with all your heart, the source of grace and
Vol - va-mos hoy a nues-tro Dios, Se - ñor de to - da

mer - cy; come seek the ten - der faith-ful-ness of
gra - cia, bus-can-do su per - dón y le - al -

1.
God.
tad.

2. Last time
God.
tad. Last time

Verse 1 / Estrofa 1

1. Now the time of grace has come, the day of sal -
1. Dí - a de la sal - va - ción, y tiem-po fa - vo -

D.C.

va - tion; come and learn now the way of our God.
ra - ble; ca - mi - ne - mos por las sen - das de Dios.

Verse 2 / Estrofa 2

2. I will take your heart of stone and place a heart with -
2. Qui-ta - ré tu co - ra - zón de pie - dra; te da-

D.C.

in you,   a heart   of com - pas - sion and   love.
ré   *un*   *co - ra - zón*   *de   a - mor y com - pas -   sión.*

Verse 3* / Estrofa 3*

3. If   you   break the   chains   of   op - pres -   sion,   if   you
   if   you   share your   bread   with the   hun -   gry,   give pro -
   give a shel - ter   to   the   home - less,   clothe the
3. *Si   tú   rom - pes   vín - cu - los   in - jus -   tos,   y a   los*
   o - fre - cien - do   pan   al ham - brien - to,   pro - tec -
   dan - do a - bri - go a quien es - tá   sin   te -   cho,   y   ves -

|1., 2.| |3.|

set the pris - 'ner   free;
tec - tion to   the   lost;
na - ked in   your   midst,   then your light   shall break
pre - sos das   li - ber - tad;
ción al   ex - tra - via - do;
ti - do al   des -   nu - do;   sur - gi - rá   tu

D.C.

forth   like   the   dawn.
luz   co - mo la au - ro - ra.

D.C.

*Soprano alone first time through repeated section, sopranos and tenors second time,
all third time.*

Text: Marty Haugen, b.1950; tr. by Ronald F. Krisman, b.1946
Tune: Marty Haugen, b.1950
© 1990, 1991, 2005, GIA Publications, Inc.

40 Si Fui Motivo de Dolor
If I Have Been the Source of Pain

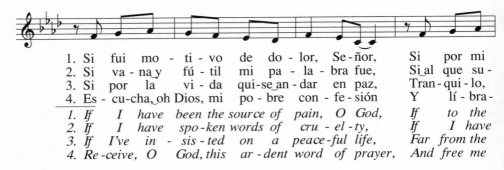

1. Si fui mo - ti - vo de do - lor, Se -ñor, Si por mi
2. Si va - na y fú - til mi pa - la - bra fue, Si al que su -
3. Si por la vi - da qui-se an - dar en paz, Tran - qui - lo,
4. Es - cu-cha, oh Dios, mi po - bre con - fe - sión Y lí - bra -

1. *If I have been the source of pain, O God, If to the*
2. *If I have spo-ken words of cru - el -ty, If I have*
3. *If I've in - sis - ted on a peace-ful life, Far from the*
4. *Re -ceive, O God, this ar -dent word of prayer, And free me*

cau - sa el dé - bil tro - pe - zó, Si en tus ca -
frí - a en su do - lor de - jé, No me con -
li - bre y sin lu - char por ti Cuan - do an - he -
me de ten - ta - ción su - til; Pre - ser - va

weak I have re - fused my strength, If in re -
left some suf - f'ring un - re - lieved, Con - demn not
strug - gles that the gos - pel brings, When you pre -
from temp - ta - tion's sub - tle snare; With ten - der

mi - nos yo no qui - se an - dar, ¡Per - dón, Se - ñor!
de - nes, tú, por mi mal - dad: ¡Per - dón, Se - ñor!
la - bas ver - me en la lid, ¡Per - dón, Se - ñor!
siem-pre mi al-ma en tu re - dil. A - mén, a - mén.

bel - lion I have strayed a - way, For - give me, God.
my in - sen - si - tiv - i - ty: For - give me, God.
fer to guide me to the strife, For - give me, God.
pa - tience, lead me to your care. A - men, a - men.

Texto: Sara Menéndez de Hall, alt., basado en un texto por C. Maude Battersby; tr. por Janet W. May, © 1992, The Pilgrim Press
Música: CAMACUÁ, 10 10 10 4; Pablo D. Sosa, n.1933, © 1988

Jesus, Remember Me / Jesús, Recuérdame   41

Ostinato Refrain / Estribillo Ostinato

Je - sus,   re - mem-ber me   when you come in - to your King - dom.
Je -sús,   re -cuér -da -me   cuan -do   en -tres en tu   Rei - no,

Je - sus,   re - mem-ber me   when you come in - to your King-dom.
Je -sús,   re - cuér -da -me,   cuan -do   en -tres en tu   Rei - no.

Text: Luke 23:42; Taizé Community, 1981; tr. by Ronald F. Krisman, b.1946
Tune: Jacques Berthier, 1923-1994
© 1981, 2005, Les Presses de Taizé, GIA Publications, Inc., agent

42 Hosanna

Refrain / Estribillo

Ho - san - na, ho - san - na! Ho -
¡Ho - san - na, ho - san - na! ¡Ho -

1.
san - na in the high - est! Ho - high - est!
san - na en el cie - lo! ¡Ho - cie - lo!

2.

Verses / Estrofas

1. Bless-ed is he, bless-ed is he; Ho -
2. Chil - dren of Je - ru - sa - lem; Ho -
3. Sing your praise, sing your praise: Ho -
1. Vi - va Je - sús, den - le ho - nor: ¡Ho -
2. Ni - ños he - bre - os, a - lé - gren - se; ¡Ho -
3. Can - ten con go - zo_un him - no triun - fal; ¡Ho -

All: Cantor:
san - na! Ho - san - na! He who comes in the
san - na! Ho - san - na! Chil - dren, wel - come
san - na! Ho - san - na! Hail the dawn of e -
san - na! ¡Ho - san - na! Él vie-ne_en nom - bre
san - na! ¡Ho - san - na! Hoy re - ci - ban a
san - na! ¡Ho - san - na! Al que nos tra - e la

All: D.S.
name of the Lord: Ho - san - na! Ho - san - na! Ho -
Christ your King; Ho - san - na! Ho - san - na! Ho -
ter - nal life; Ho - san - na! Ho - san - na! Ho -
del Se - ñor; ¡Ho - san - na! ¡Ho - san - na! ¡Ho -
Cris - to Rey: ¡Ho - san - na! ¡Ho - san - na! ¡Ho -
vi - da_in-mor-tal: ¡Ho - san - na! ¡Ho - san - na! ¡Ho -

Text: Scott Soper, b.1961; tr. by Ronald F. Krisman, b.1946
Tune: Scott Soper, b.1961
© 1997, 2005, GIA Publications, Inc.

Lift High the Cross / Alcen la Cruz   43

Refrain / Estribillo

Lift high the cross, the love of Christ pro-claim till
Al - cen la cruz, em - ble - ma de su_a-mor; que_el

all the world a - dore his sa - cred name.
mun-do_al fin co - noz - ca_al Sal - va - dor.

Verses / Estrofas

1. Come, Chris - tians, fol - low where the Mas - ter trod, Our
2. Led on their way by this tri - um-phant sign, The
3. Each new - born fol - l'wer of the Cru - ci - fied Bears
4. O Lord, once lift - ed on the glo - rious tree, Your

1. *Va - mos, cris - tia - nos, tras nues-tro Se - ñor; El*
2. *Ba - jo_es - te sig - no de su gran po - der El*
3. *Ca - da cre-yen - te del que_en cruz mu - rió En*
4. *Cuan - do te_al-za - ron glo - rio-so_en la cruz, A -*

D.C.

King vic - to - rious, Christ, the Son of God.
hosts of God in con - quering ranks com - bine.
on the brow the seal of him who died.
death has bought us life e - ter - nal - ly.

rey vic-to-rio - so, Cris - to,_Hi - jo de Dios.
pue - blo de Dios a - van - za sin te - mer.
su fren-te lle - va_el sig - no_en que ven - ció.
llí pro-me-tis - te lle-var - nos a la luz.

5. So shall our song of triumph ever be: 5. *Himnos de gloria_alcemos sin cesar;*
   Praise to the Crucified for victory!   *Al rey vencedor que_en cruz supo triunfar.*

Text: 1 Corinthians 1:18; George W. Kitchin, 1827-1912, and Michael R. Newbolt, 1874-1956, alt.; tr. by Dimas Planas-Belfort, 1934-1992,
   and Ángel Mattos, alt.
Tune: CRUCIFER, 10 10 with refrain; Sydney H. Nicholson, 1875-1947
© 1974, 1997, Hope Publishing Co.

44 El Señor Nos Ama Hoy
Christ Our Lord Has Loved Us

Estribillo / Refrain

"Es   mi cuer-po: to-mad y co-med. Es   mi san - gre: to-
"This is my bod - y,   take and   eat.   This is my pre-cious blood,

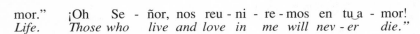

mad   y be-bed. Por-que yo soy la vi - da,   yo soy el a-
take   and drink. For   I am the Res - ur - rec-tion and the

mor."   ¡Oh Se - ñor, nos reu - ni - re -mos en tu_a - mor!
Life.   Those who   live and love in   me will nev - er   die."

Estrofas / Verses

1.-3. El   Se - ñor nos a - ma hoy Co - mo na - die   nos a - mó.
1.-3. Christ our Lord has loved us more   Than all love we've known be -fore,

Él   nos guí - a co-mo_un fa - ro   en un mar de_os-cu - ri - dad.
Y   tan gran-de fue su_a-mor que   lo con - du-jo_has-ta la cruz.
En   la cruz el Sal - va - dor su   pro - pia vi - da nos do - nó.
And   he guides us like a light-house through a night of rag -ing storm.
With a love so great it led him   to his death up - on the cross.
From the cross, our Sav - ior of - fers us his own a -bun-dant life.

Jun - tos   al   co - mer el Pan, Él nos brin - da su_a-mis-tad.
Pe - ro   más pu-do_el a - mor   que la muer-te_y el do - lor:
Por su_Es-pí - ri - tu en-tra - mos al Cuer - po del Se - ñor.
When we   join in faith to eat,   he be-comes the Host we greet
Such a   love in-spires be -lief strong-er still than death and grief.
Spir - it-blessed, we are re-born   as   the Bod - y   of our Lord,

D.C.

Es el Pan de Dios, el Pan de la unidad.
Al pasar tres días Él resucitó.
Nada puede separarnos de su amor.

In the Bread of Life, the Bread of Unity.
After three days he arises from the grave.
And no pow'r can separate us from his love.

4. El Señor nos ama hoy como nadie nos amó.
   "Donde dos o tres personas, inspiradas por mi amor,
   Se reunen para orar, estaré presente yo."
   Esta fue la fiel promesa del Señor.

5. El Señor nos ama hoy como nadie nos amó.
   "El mayor entre ustedes debe ser como el menor.
   He lavado hoy tus pies, aunque soy tu buen Señor.
   Hagan esto en memoria de mi amor."

6. El Señor nos ama hoy como nadie nos amó.
   "Los que tengan hambre y sed vendrán a mí, y los saciaré,
   Pues yo soy el vivo Pan y agua que no da más sed,
   Y por siempre en sus vidas moraré."

4. *Christ our Lord has loved us more than all love we've known before:*
   "And where two or three are gathered in the Spirit of my love,
   When you join your hearts to pray, I am in your midst that day."
   Hear the faithful promise spoken by our Lord.

5. *Christ our Lord has loved us more than all love we've known before:*
   "For the first among you shall become the lowliest of all.
   As I kneel to wash your feet, serve all others whom you meet,
   Acting always in the mem'ry of my love."

6. *Christ our Lord has loved us more than all love we've known before:*
   "All the hungry and the parching shall be filled and satisfied.
   Like the manna God dispersed, Living Waters quenching thirst:
   I shall dwell within your hearts forevermore."

Texto: Anónimo; tr. por Mary Louise Bringle, n.1953, © 2005, GIA Publications, Inc.
Música: BY AND BY, 7 7 15 7 7 11 con estribillo; Charles A. Tindley, 1851-1933, alt.; arm. por Ronald F. Krisman, n.1946, © 2005, GIA Publications, Inc.

45 Jesu, Jesu / Jesús, Jesús

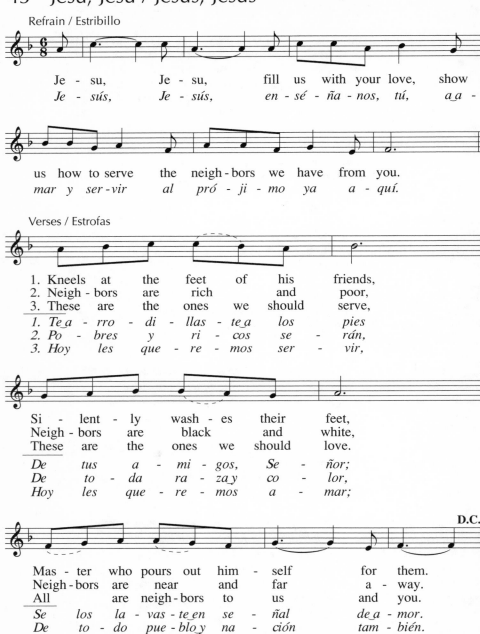

Refrain / Estribillo

Je - su, Je - su, fill us with your love, show
Je - sús, *Je - sús,* *en - sé - ña - nos, tú,* *a a -*

us how to serve the neigh-bors we have from you.
mar y ser-vir al pró - ji - mo ya a - quí.

Verses / Estrofas

1. Kneels at the feet of his friends,
2. Neigh - bors are rich and poor,
3. These are the ones we should serve,

1. Te a - rro - di - llas - te a los pies
2. Po - bres y ri - cos se - rán,
3. Hoy les que - re - mos ser - vir,

Si - lent - ly wash - es their feet,
Neigh - bors are black and white,
These are the ones we should love.

De tus a - mi - gos, Se - ñor;
De to - da ra - za y co - lor,
Hoy les que - re - mos a - mar;

D.C.

Mas - ter who pours out him - self for them.
Neigh-bors are near and far a - way.
All are neigh-bors to us and you.

Se los la - vas - te en se - ñal de a - mor.
De to - do pue - blo y na - ción tam - bién.
So - mos i - gua - les, Je - sús, en ti.

4. Kneel at the feet of our friends,
   Silently washing their feet,
   This is the way we should live with you.

4. Nuestra rodilla doblar
   Y así sus pies lavar,
   Es el mandato que Dios nos da.

Text: Tom Colvin, 1925-2000; tr. by Felicia Fina, alt.
Tune: CHEREPONI, Irregular with refrain; Ghana folk song; adapt. by Tom Colvin, 1925-2000; acc. by Jane M. Marshall, b.1924
© 1969, arr. and trans., © 1982, Hope Publishing Co.

Venid, Oh Cristianos   46
O Come, Let Us Worship

Estribillo / Refrain

Ve - nid, oh cris - tia - nos, la cruz a - do - re - mos, La
O come, let us wor - ship the cross of Christ Je - sus, The

cruz en - sal - ce - mos que al mun - do sal - vó.
tree on which hung the world's Sav - ior and Lord.

Estrofas / Verses

1. Di - cho - sa a - que - lla al - ma Que tie - ne pre - sen - te
2. ¡Oh cruz a - do - ra - ble! Te a - mo y te a - do - ro,
3. Re - ci - be, cruz san - ta, Mis bra - zos can - sa - dos,
4. Ve - nid, al - mas fie - les, Be - sad con an - he - lo,

1. We hum - bly ap - proach you With deep - est de - vo - tion.
2. O cross, rich and won - drous, We love and a - dore you.
3. Re - ceive, cross most ho - ly, Our arms, weak and wea - ry,
4. As faith - ful be - liev - ers, Our lips touch you gen - tly,

D.C.

A quien con ar - dien - te a - fec - to la a - mó.
Cual ri - co te - so - ro de gra - cia y de a - mor.
Y en ti re - cli - na - dos al - can - cen a Dios.
La lla - ve del cie - lo, la cruz del Se - ñor.

Re - mem - ber us, Lord, in your king - dom of peace.
What treas - ures you of - fer of grace and of love!
Out - stretched toward your mer - cy, and rest - ing in you.
The key to the heav - ens, the cross of our Lord.

5. Amemos, cristianos,
   La cruz del amado
   Jesús, que enclavado
   en ella murió.

6. Permite que llegue
   A ti, y que muera;
   ¡Cuán dulce me fuera
   lograr tal favor!

5. Recall how the Body
   Of Christ, our Beloved,
   Was nailed to a tree,
   where he suffered and died.

6. Lord, help us to enter
   Your tree's holy myst'ry:
   To die to ourselves
   and abide in your peace.

Texto: Tradicional; tr. por Mary Louise Bringle, n.1953, © 2005, GIA Publications, Inc.
Música: Tradicional; arm. por Ronald F. Krisman, n.1946, © 2005, GIA Publications, Inc.

47 Were You There
¿Presenciaste la Muerte del Señor?

1. Were you there when they cru - ci - fied my Lord?
2. Were you there when they nailed him to the tree?
3. Were you there when they pierced him in the side?

1. *¿Pre - sen - cias - te la muer - te del Se - ñor?*
2. *¿Vis - te cuan - do en la cruz cla - va - do fue?*
3. *¿Vis - te cuan - do su es - pí - ri - tu en - tre - gó?*

Were you there when they cru - ci - fied my Lord?
Were you there when they nailed him to the tree?
Were you there when they pierced him in the side?

¿Pre - sen - cias - te la muer - te del Se - ñor?
¿Vis - te cuan - do en la cruz cla - va - do fue?
¿Vis - te cuan - do su es - pí - ri - tu en - tre - gó?

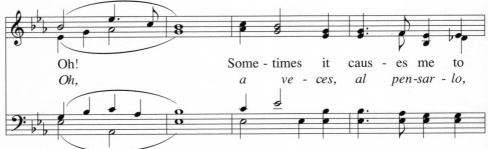

Oh! Some - times it caus - es me to
Oh, a ve - ces, al pen-sar - lo,

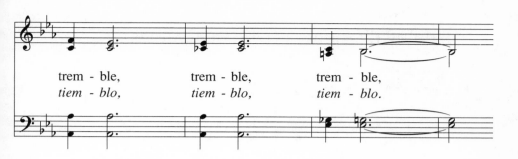

trem - ble,   trem - ble,   trem - ble,
tiem - blo,   *tiem - blo,*   *tiem - blo.*

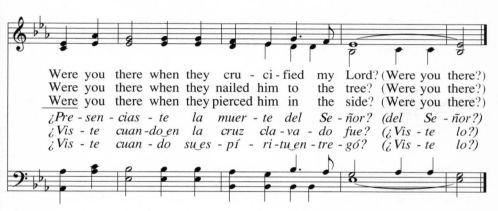

Were you there when they cru - ci - fied my Lord? (Were you there?)
Were you there when they nailed him to the tree? (Were you there?)
Were you there when they pierced him in the side? (Were you there?)
¿Pre - sen - cias - te la muer - te del Se - ñor? (del Se - ñor?)
¿Vis - te cuan - do en la cruz cla - va - do fue? (¿Vis - te lo?)
¿Vis - te cuan - do su es - pí - ri - tu en - tre - gó? (¿Vis - te lo?)

4. Were you there
     when the sun refused to shine?
  Were you there
     when the sun refused to shine?
  Oh! Sometimes it causes me to
     tremble, tremble, tremble,
  Were you there
     when the sun refused to shine?
       (Were you there?)

4. *¿Viste cuando*
     el sol se oscureció?
  ¿Viste cuando
     el sol se oscureció?
  Oh, a veces, al pensarlo,
     tiemblo, tiemblo, tiemblo.
  ¿Viste cuando
     el sol se oscureció?
       (¿Viste lo?)

5. Were you there
     when they laid him in the tomb?
  Were you there
     when they laid him in the tomb?
  Oh! Sometimes it causes me to
     tremble, tremble, tremble,
  Were you there
     when they laid him in the tomb?
       (Were you there?)

5. *¿Viste cuando*
     la tumba le encerró?
  ¿Viste cuando
     la tumba le encerró?
  Oh, a veces, al pensarlo,
     tiemblo, tiemblo, tiemblo.
  ¿Viste cuando
     la tumba le encerró?
       (¿Viste lo?)

Text: African-American spiritual; tr. sts. 1, 2, 4, 5 by Federico J. Pagura, b.1923, alt., ©; st. 3 tr. by Lois Kroehler, © 1970
Tune: WERE YOU THERE, 10 10 with refrain; African-American spiritual; harm. by Robert J. Batastini, b.1942, © 1987, GIA Publications, Inc.

48 Alleluia No. 1
¡Aleluya! ¡Aleluya! Demos Gracias

Refrain / Estribillo

Descant:
Al - le - lu - ia, al - le -
¡A - le - lu - ya! ja - le -

Melody:
Al - le - lu - ia, al - le - lu - ia, give thanks to the
¡A - le - lu - ya! ja - le - lu - ya! de - mos gra - cias a

lu - ia, al - le - lu - ia,
lu - ya! a - le - lu - ya, a - la -

ris - en Lord. Al - le - lu - ia, al - le - lu - ia, give
Cris - to Rey. A - le - lu - ya, a - le - lu - ya, a - la -

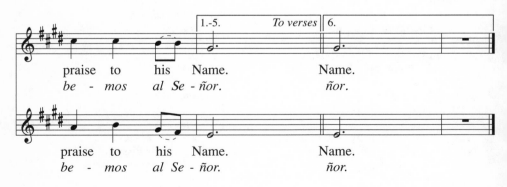

1.-5.   *To verses*   6.

praise to his Name.   Name.
be - mos al Se - ñor.   ñor.

praise to his Name.   Name.
be - mos al Se - ñor.   ñor.

Verses / Estrofas

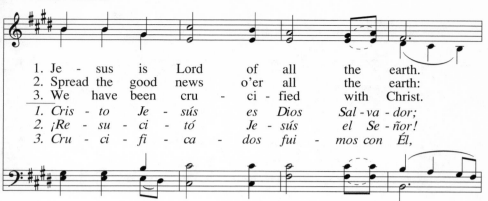

1. Je - sus is Lord of all the earth.
2. Spread the good news o'er all the earth:
3. We have been cru - ci - fied with Christ.

1. Cris - to Je - sús es Dios Sal - va - dor;
2. ¡Re - su - ci - tó Je - sús el Se - ñor!
3. Cru - ci - fi - ca - dos fui - mos con Él,

D.C.

He is the King of cre - a - tion.
Je - sus has died and has ris - en.
Now we shall live for ev - er.

Del u - ni - ver - so es Rey y Se - ñor.
La bue - na nue - va_a - nun - cie - mos do -quier.
Mas vi - vi - re - mos por la_e - ter -ni - dad.

D.C.

4. God has proclaimed his gracious gift:
   Life eternal for all who believe.

4. Dios prometió a la_humanidad
   Vida_abundante_y su don celestial.

5. Come, let us praise the living God,
   Joyfully sing to our Savior.

5. Vengan, cantemos al Salvador
   Himnos que_alaben su gran majestad.

Text: Donald Fishel, b.1950, © 1973, Word of God Music
Tune: ALLELUIA NO. 1, 8 8 with refrain; Donald Fishel, b.1950, © 1973, Word of God Music; descant harm. by Betty Pulkingham, b.1928,
    Charles Mallory, b.1953, and George Mims, b.1938, © 1979, Celebration

49   Shepherd Me, O God / Guíame, Señor

Refrain / Estribillo

mp

Shep-herd me, O God, be - yond my wants, be -
Guí - a - me, Se - ñor, mi buen Pas - tor; con -

mp

Shep-herd me, be - yond my wants, be -
Guí - a - me, mi buen Pas - tor; con -

To verses 1, 2, 3 | To verse 4

yond my fears, from death in-to life. life.
dú - ce - me de la muer-te_a la vi-da. vi-da.

yond my fears, from death to life. life.
dú - ce - me de la muer-te_a la vi-da. vi-da.

Verses 1-3 / Estrofas 1-3

1. God is my shep-herd, so noth-ing shall I want, I rest in the
2. Gen - tly you raise me and heal my wea-ry soul, you lead me by
3. Though I should wan-der the val - ley of death, I fear no

1. *Tú_e-res mi pas - tor, y na - da me fal-ta: en ver-des pra-*
2. *Cuán tier-na - men-te mi al - ma for-ta-le-ces; por siem-pre me*
3. *Aun - que ca - mi-ne por ca - ña - das os-cu-ras, ʼ no te-mo*

mead-ows of faith-ful-ness and love, I walk by the
path - ways of right-eous-ness and truth, my spir - it shall
e - vil, for you are at my side, your rod and your

de - ras me ha-ces re - po - sar. Ha - cia fuen - tes tran-
guí - as por sen-das de ver - dad; se_a - le - gra mi_es-
na - da, por - que tú vas con-mi-go. Tu va-ra_y tu ca -

D.C.

qui - et wa - ters of peace.
sing the mu - sic of your name.
staff, my com - fort and my hope.
qui - las me quie - res con - du - cir.
pí - ri - tu en tu san - to nom - bre.
ya - do: e - llos me so - sie - gan.

Verse 4 / Estrofa 4

ff

4. You have set me a ban-quet of love in the face of
4. *Tú pre-pa-ras u-na me-sa an-te mí, en-fren-te de mis e-ne-*

pp unis.

rit. D.C.

ha - tred, crown-ing me with love be-yond my pow'r to hold.
mi - gos; me un-ges la ca - be-za, y mi co-pa re - bo-sa.

Verse 5 / Estrofa 5

p

5. Sure - ly your kind - ness and mer - cy fol-low me
5. *Me a-com-pa - ña - rán tu bon - dad y tu mer -ced*

poco rit. *a tempo*

all the days of my life; I will dwell in the house of my
to - dos los dí - as de mi vi - da. Ha-bi-ta - ré en la ca -sa del Se -

God for ev - er - more.
ñor por a - ños sin tér - mi - no.

Final Refrain / Estribillo Final

p *a bit slower*

Shep-herd me, O God, be - yond my wants, be -
Guí - a - me, Se - ñor, mi buen Pas - tor; con -

yond my fears, from death in - to life.
dú - ce - me de la muer-te a la vi - da.

Text: Psalm 23; Marty Haugen, b.1950; tr. by Ronald F. Krisman, b.1946
Tune: Marty Haugen, b.1950

50 El Peregrino de Emaús
The Emmaus Road

Estrofas / Verses

1. "¿Qué lle - va - bas con - ver - san - do?" me di - jis - te, buen a -
2. Van tres dí - as que se ha muer - to y se a - ca - ba mi es - pe -
3. "¡Qué tar - dí - os co - ra - zo - nes, qué ig-no - ran - cia a los pro -
4. Hi - zo se - ñas de se - guir más a - llá de nues-tra al -

1. "Tell me, friends, why look so trou - bled in your anx-ious con - ver -
2. He's been dead for near - ly three days; and my hopes, as well, are
3. "Fool-ish peo - ple!" he re - spond-ed, "slow of heart in your be -
4. He be - gan to trav-el on-ward, as the west-ern sun was

mi - go. Y me de - tu - ve a - som - bra - do a la
ran - za. Di - cen que al - gu - nas mu - je - res al se -
fe - tas! Se a - nun - ció en pro - fe - cí - a que el Me -
de - a. Ya la luz del sol po - nien - te pa - re -

sa - tion?" At these words, I stopped, a - ston-ished by the
dy - ing. Though I've heard a group of wom-en sought his
liev - ing How the proph-ets all fore-told this; yet in -
set - ting. We in - vit - ed him to join us and to

ve - ra del ca - mi - no. ¿No sa - bes lo que ha pa -
pul - cro fue - ron de al - ba. Di - je - ron que al - gu - nos
sí - as pa - de - cie - ra, Y por lle - gar a su
cí - a que mu - rie - ra. "Qué - da - te, fo - ras -

stran - ger's kind - ly ques - tion. Don't you know what just
tomb this ver - y morn-ing. They said they heard an - gels'
stead, you stand here griev-ing! Be - fore He could en - ter
share a ta - ble bless-ing. Our eyes all at once were

sa - do a - yer en Je - ru - sa - lén, De Je -
o - tros lo bus - ca - ban a - llá tam - bién. Mas se a -
glo - ria es - co - gie - ra la a - flic - ción." En la
te - ro; pon - te a la me - sa y ben - di - ce." Y al des-
hap-pened on a hill near Je - ru - sa - lem: Where they
voic - es who an-nounced that he was a - live. But no
glo - ry, the Mes - si - ah must suf - fer loss." At these
o - pened, though he van - ished from our sight. We had

sús, el Na - za - re - no, a quien cla - va - ron en
ca - ba mi con - fian - za: no en - con - tra - ron a Je -
tar - de de a - quél dí - a, yo sen - tí que con Je -
te - llo de su luz, en la ben - di - ción del
cru - ci - fied one Je - sus, shed-ding pure and sin - less
one has found his bod - y, and my fear - ful doubts have
words our hearts were burn-ing hear - ing Scrip-ture's truth un -
seen our Friend and Sav - ior in the bread he blessed and

cruz? Por e - so me vuel - vo tris - te a mi al -
sús. Por e - so me vuel - vo tris - te a mi al -
sús Nues - tro co - ra - zón ar - dí - a a la
pan, Mis o - jos re - co - no - cie - ron al A -
blood? For this rea - son, I am dis - heart-ened as I
grown. For this rea - son, I am dis - heart-ened as I
fold. So we urged him to ling - er with us res - ting
broke. Then we knew that the Christ had ris - en for He

de - a de E - ma - ús.
de - a de E - ma - ús.
vis - ta de E - ma - ús.
mi - go de E - ma - ús.
walk the Em - ma - us Road.
walk the Em - ma - us Road.
by the Em - ma - us Road.
graced the Em - ma - us Road.

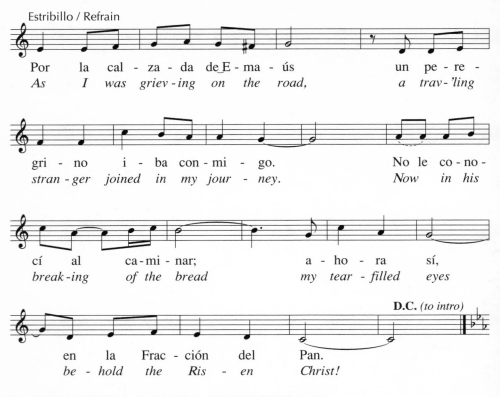

Estribillo / Refrain

Por la cal - za - da de E - ma - ús un pe - re -
As I was griev - ing on the road, *a trav - 'ling*

gri - no i - ba con - mi - go. No le co - no -
stran - ger joined in my jour - ney. *Now in his*

cí al ca - mi - nar; a - ho - ra sí,
break - ing of the bread *my tear - filled eyes*

D.C. *(to intro)*

en la Frac - ción del Pan.
be - hold the Ris - en Christ!

Texto: Rafael Jiménez, siglo XX; tr. por Mary Louise Bringle, n.1953, © 2005, GIA Publications, Inc.
Música: *Misa Panamericana;* "Los Perales"; arm. por Ronald F. Krisman, n.1946, © 2005, GIA Publications, Inc.

51 O Sons and Daughters
Alzad, Oh Pueblos, Vuestra Voz

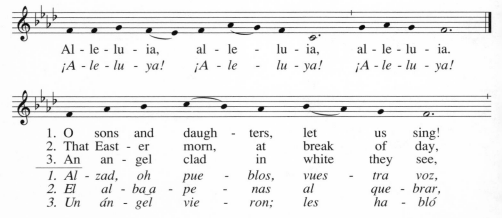

Al - le - lu - ia, al - le - lu - ia, al - le - lu - ia.
¡A - le - lu - ya! ¡A - le - lu - ya! ¡A - le - lu - ya!

1. O sons and daugh - ters, let us sing!
2. That East - er morn, at break of day,
3. An an - gel clad in white they see,
1. *Al - zad, oh pue - blos, vues - tra voz,*
2. *El al - ba_a - pe - nas al que - brar,*
3. *Un án - gel vie - ron; les ha - bló*

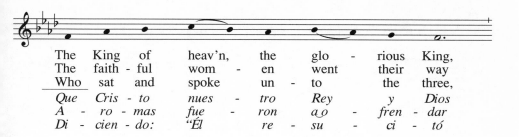

The King of heav'n, the glo - rious King,
The faith - ful wom - en went their way
Who sat and spoke un - to the three,
Que Cris - to nues - tro Rey y Dios
A - ro - mas fue - ron a_o - fren - dar
Di - cien - do: "Él re - su - ci - tó

D.C.

O'er death to - day rose tri - umph-ing. Al - le - lu - ia!
To seek the tomb where Je - sus lay. Al - le - lu - ia!
"Your Lord has gone to Gal - i - lee." Al - le - lu - ia!
Ven - ció la muer - te_y su te - rror. ¡A - le - lu - ya!
Mu - je - res fie - les, con pie - dad. ¡A - le - lu - ya!
Y_a Ga - li - le - a ya mar -chó." ¡A - le - lu - ya!

4. That night the apostles met in fear;
   Amidst them came their Lord most dear,
   And said, "My peace be on all here."
   Alleluia!

5. When Thomas first the tidings heard,
   How they had seen the risen Lord,
   He doubted the disciples' word.
   Alleluia!

6. "My wounded side, O Thomas, see;
   Behold my hands, my feet," said he,
   "Not faithless, but believing be."
   Alleluia!

7. No longer Thomas then denied,
   He saw the feet, the hands, the side;
   "You are my Lord and God," he cried.
   Alleluia!

8. How blest are they who have not seen,
   And yet whose faith has constant been,
   For they eternal life shall win.
   Alleluia!

9. On this most holy day of days,
   To God your hearts and voices raise,
   In laud, and jubilee and praise.
   Alleluia!

4. *Aquella noche con temor,*
   Reunidos todos, el Señor
   Les dijo: "Paz, mi paz les doy."
   ¡Aleluya!

5. *La grata nueva_oyó Tomás:*
   "El Cristo vive, cerca_está."
   Mas no la pudo aceptar.
   ¡Aleluya!

6. *"Mis manos mira, oh Tomás,*
   Y mis heridas toca ya;
   Confía_en mí, no dudes más."
   ¡Aleluya!

7. *Con reverencia_y con temor*
   Cayó Tomás ante_el Señor,
   Y dijo: "Eres tú mi Dios."
   ¡Aleluya!

8. *"Los que no_han visto_y pueden creer,*
   Benditos son y_habrán de ser,
   Pues vida_eterna les daré."
   ¡Aleluya!

9. *En este día del Señor,*
   A Dios alzad el corazón,
   Con alegría_y con amor.
   ¡Aleluya!

Text: *O filii et filiae;* Jean Tisserand, d.1494; English tr. by John M. Neale, 1818-1866, alt.; Spanish tr. by Federico J. Pagura, b.1923, © 1962
Tune: O FILII ET FILIAE, 888 with alleluias; Mode II; acc. by Richard Proulx, b.1937, © 1975, GIA Publications, Inc.

52 O Holy Dove of God Descending
Paloma Santa, Descendiendo

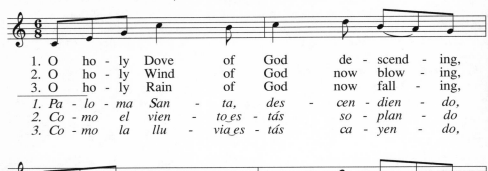

1. O ho-ly Dove of God de-scend-ing,
2. O ho-ly Wind of God now blow-ing,
3. O ho-ly Rain of God now fall-ing,

1. Pa-lo-ma San-ta, des-cen-dien-do,
2. Co-mo el vien-to es-tás so-plan-do
3. Co-mo la llu-via es-tás ca-yen-do,

You are the love that knows no end-ing,
You are the seed that God is sow-ing,
You make the Word of God en-thrall-ing,

A-las de a-mor me es-tán cu-brien-do,
Y la se-mi-lla es-tás sem-bran-do,
Qui-tas la sed que es-toy te-nien-do,

All of our shat-tered dreams you're mend-ing:
You are the life that starts us grow-ing:
You are that in-ner voice now call-ing:

Tu dul-ce paz es-tás tra-yen-do;
Mi fe es-ca-sa es-tá bro-tan-do;
Con el a-mor me es-tás un-gien-do;

Spir-it, now live in me.
Spir-it, now live in me.
Spir-it, now live in me.

Mo-ra en mi vi-vir.
Mo-ra en mi vi-vir.
Mo-ra en mi vi-vir.

4. O holy Flame of God now burning,
   You are the power of Christ returning,
   You are the answer to our yearning:
   Spirit, now live in me.

4. *Como un fuego estás ardiendo,*
   Mi corazón estás fundiendo,
   Llama de luz estás prendiendo;
   Mora en mi vivir.

Text: Bryan Jeffery Leech, b.1931, © 1976, Fred Bock Music Co.; tr. by Barbara Mink, b.1937, © 1987
Tune: LOIS, 9 9 9 6; Bryan Jeffery Leech, b.1931, © 1976, Fred Bock Music Co.

Soplo del Dios Viviente 53
Breath of the Living God

Estrofas / Verses

1. So - plo del Dios vi - vien - te que en el prin -
2. So - plo del Dios vi - vien - te por quien el
3. So - plo del Dios vi - vien - te por quien na -
1. *Breath of the liv - ing God, who in the be -*
2. *Breath of the liv - ing God, whose e - ter - nal*
3. *Breath of the liv - ing God, source of life a -*

ci - pio cu - bris-te el a - gua; So - plo del Dios vi -
Ver - bo se hi - zo car - ne, So - plo del Dios vi -
ce - mos en el bau - tis - mo; So - plo del Dios vi -
gin - ning moved o'er the wa - ters, Breath of the liv - ing
Word came to dwell a - mong us, Breath of the liv - ing
new through our ho - ly Bap - tism, Breath of the liv - ing

vien - te que fe - cun - das - te la cre - a - ción.
vien - te que re - no - vas - te la cre - a - ción.
vien - te que con - sa - gras - te la cre - a - ción.
God, by whom all cre - a - tion was first con - ceived.
God, by whom all cre - a - tion has been re - newed.
God, by whom all cre - a - tion is sanc - ti - fied.

Estribillo / Refrain

¡Ven hoy a nues-tras vi - das, in - fún-de-nos tus do - nes!
Come now and live with - in us, come, let your gifts en - rich us,

So - plo del Dios vi - vien - te, oh San-to Es-pí - ri-tu Cre - a - dor!
Breath of the liv - ing God, our Cre - a - tor Spir - it, e - ter-nal Source.

Texto: Osvaldo Catena, 1920-1986, alt., © 1979, Editorial Bonum; tr. por *The New Century Hymnal,* © 1993, Pilgrim Press
Música: DIOS VIVIENTE, 7 10 7 9 con estribillo; Tradicional de Noruega; arm. por Lorraine Florindez, © 1991, Editorial Concordia

54 Send Us Your Spirit
Señor, Envía Tu Espíritu Santo

Refrain / Estribillo

Come Lord Je - sus, send us your Spir - it, re -
¡Se - ñor, en - ví - a tu Es - pí - ri - tu San - to! Re -

new the face of the earth.
nue - va la faz de la tie - rra. ¡Se -

Come Lord Je - sus, send us your Spir - it, re -
ñor, en - ví - a tu Es - pí - ri - tu San - to! Re -

new the face of the earth.
nue - va la faz de la tie - rra.

To verses | Final ending

Verses / Estrofas

1. Come to us, Spir - it of God,
2. Fill us with the fire of your love,
3. Send us the wings of new birth,

1. San - to Es - pí - ri - tu, ven,
2. Ven con el fue - go de tu a - mor,
3. Da - nos un re - na - ci - mien - to,

*May be sung in canon.

breathe in us now, we sing to - geth - er.
burn in us now, bring us to - geth - er.
fill all the earth with the love you have taught us.
so - pla en no - so - tros: jun - tos can - ta - mos.
ar - de en no - so - tros. Re - ú - ne - nos to - dos.
Lle - na la tie - rra de tu a -mor pro - me - ti - do.

Spir - it of hope and of
Come to us, dwell in us,
Let all cre - a - tion
Da - dor de la luz y es - pe -
Ha - bi - ta en no - so - tros, trans -
Que to - da la cre - a -

light, fill our lives,
change our lives, O Lord,
now be shak - en with love,
ran - za, sá - cia - nos. ¡Es -
fór - ma -nos por tu po - der. ¡Es -
ción se mue - va por ti. ¡Es -

D.C.

come to us, Spir - it of God.
come to us, Spir - it of God.
come to us, Spir - it of God.
pí - ri - tu San - to, ven!
pí - ri - tu San - to, ven!
pí - ri - tu San - to, ven!

Text: David Haas, b.1957; tr. by Ronald F. Krisman, b.1946
Tune: David Haas, b.1957; acc. by Jeanne Cotter, b.1964
© 1981, 1982, 1987, 2005, GIA Publications, Inc.

55 Gracias por el Amor
Thank You for Love

1. Gra - cias por el a - mor del cie - lo.
2. Gra - cias por el a - mor del mun - do.
3. Gra - cias por es - te nue - vo dí - a.
1. Thank you for love you send from heav - en.
2. Thank you for lov - ing all cre - a - tion.
3. Thank you for mer - cies new each morn - ing.

Gra - cias por el in - men - so mar. Gra - cias por el can -
Gra - cias por la fe - li - ci - dad. Gra - cias por to - da
Gra - cias por nues - tra ju - ven - tud. Gra - cias por la a - mis -
Thank you for vast and roll - ing seas. Thank you for fields and
Thank you for joys that fill the earth. Thank you for the em -
Thank you for child - hood days and youth. Thank you for friend - ships

tar del bos - que. A - le - lu - ya.
mi fa - mi - lia. A - le - lu - ya.
tad de to - dos. A - le - lu - ya.
wood - lands sing - ing Al - le - lu - ia.
brace of fam - 'ly: Al - le - lu - ia.
that de - light us: Al - le - lu - ia.

4. Gracias por toda la hermosura.
Gracias por nuestra gran unión.
Gracias por todas las bondades.
Aleluya.

4. Thank you for all you touch with beauty.
Thank you for joining hearts as one.
Thank you for all your goodness to us:
Alleluia.

5. Gracias por tu venida al mundo.
Gracias por tu misión de paz.
Gracias porque has unido el tiempo
Con la eternidad.

5. Thank you for being born among us.
Thank you for bearing gifts of peace.
Thank you for wedding earthly time with
Your eternity.

Texto: Anónimo; tr. por Mary Louise Bringle, n.1953, © 2005, GIA Publications, Inc.
Música: Tradicional; arm. por Ronald F. Krisman, n.1946, © 2005, GIA Publications, Inc.

Praise and Thanksgiving 56
Te Damos Gracias por Cuanto Has Hecho

1. Praise and thanks - giv - ing, Fa - ther, we of - fer,
2. Lord, bless the la - bor We bring to serve you,
3. Fa - ther, pro - vid - ing Food for your chil - dren,
4. Then will your bless - ing Reach ev - 'ry peo - ple,

1. *¡Te da - mos gra - cias Por cuan-to_has he - cho,*
2. *¡Ben - di - ce_oh Cris - to, Lo que tra - e - mos;*
3. *¡Oh, Pa - ra - cle - to Que_a-quíen la tie - rra*
4. *Y_a - sí que_al - can - ce Tu_a - mor a to - dos,*

For all things liv - ing You have made good:
That with our neigh - bor We may be fed.
By your wise guid - ing Teach us to share
Free - ly con - fess - ing Your gra - cious hand.

Oh Pa - dre_e - ter - no, En tu bon - dad:
Díg - na - te_a to - dos A - li - men - tar!
A to - dos cui - das Con tu bon - dad:
Y tus pie - da - des Ben - de - ci - rán.

Har - vest of sown fields, Fruits of the or - chard,
Sow - ing or till - ing, We would work with you,
One with an - oth - er, So that, re - joic - ing
Where you are reign - ing No one will hun - ger,

Nues - tras co - se - chas, Fru - tos del cam - po
Ben - di - ce_a cuan - tos Jun - to con - ti - go
Que_u - nos y o - tros, Jun - tos o - bre - mos
Ba - jo tu rei - no Na - die ca - re - ce:

Hay from the mown fields, Blos - som and wood.
Har - vest - ing, mill - ing, For dai - ly bread.
With us, all oth - ers May know your care.
Your love sus - tain - ing, Fruit - ful the land.

Con que co - ro - nas Nues -tra_he - re - dad!
El pan pro - cu - ran Mul - ti - pli - car.
Co - mo_ins - tru - men - tos De tu pie - dad!
Tu_a - mor fe - cun - do Nos brin - da pan.

Text: Albert F. Bayly, 1901-1984, © Oxford University Press; tr. by Dimas Planas-Belfort,1934-1992, alt., © 1989, Editorial Avance Luterano
Tune: BUNESSAN, 5 5 5 4 D; Scots Gaelic; harm. by A. Gregory Murray, OSB, 1905-1992, © Downside Abbey

57 We Gather Together / Nos Hemos Reunido

1. We gath - er to - geth - er to ask the Lord's bless - ing;
2. Be - side us to guide us, our God with us join - ing,
3. We all do ex - tol you our lead - er tri - um - phant,

1. Nos he - mos reu - ni - do en el nom - bre de Cris - to
2. Nos has pro - te - gi - do en nues - tro sen - de - ro,
3. Tu nom - bre a - la - ba - mos, Se - ñor vic - to - rio - so;

He chas - tens and has - tens his will to make known;
Whose king - dom calls all to the love which en - dures.
And pray that you still our de - fend - er will be.

Pa - ra a - gra - de - cer tus bon - da - des, oh Dios.
Nos has cir - cun - da - do de bie - nes y ho - nor;
En to - das las lu - chas con - cé - de - nos paz;

The wick - ed op - press - ing now cease from dis - tress - ing
So from the be - gin - ning the fight we were win - ning;
Let your con - gre - ga - tion es - cape trib - u - la - tion:

Con mu - chos cui - da - dos nos has so - co - rri - do.
Por e - so, Dios san - to, tu pue - blo reu - ni - do
Tu a - mor nos am - pa - re, tu rei - no nos ven - ga;

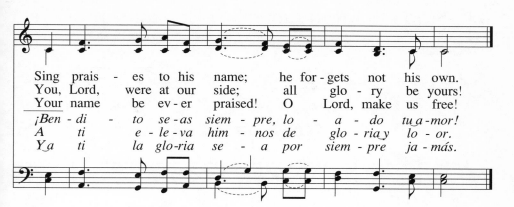

Sing prais - es to his name; he for - gets not his own.
You, Lord, were at our side; all glo - ry be yours!
Your name be ev - er praised! O Lord, make us free!
¡Ben - di - to se - as siem - pre, lo - a - do tu a -mor!
A ti e - le - va him - nos de glo - ria y lo - or.
Ya ti la glo -ria se - a por siem - pre ja - más.

Text: *Wilt heden nu treden,* Netherlands folk hymn; English tr. by Theodore Baker, 1851-1934, alt.; Spanish tr. by Juanita R. de Balloch, b.1894
Tune: KREMSER, 12 11 12 11; *Nederlandtsch Gedenck-clanck,* 1626; harm. by Edward Kremser, 1838-1914

58 Si Yo No Tengo Amor / If I Do Not Have Love

Estribillo / Refrain

Si yo no ten-go_a-mor, yo na - da soy, Se-ñor.
If I do not have love, then I am noth-ing, Lord.

Si yo no ten-go_a - mor, yo na - da soy, Se - ñor.
If I do not have love, then I am noth-ing, Lord.

Estrofas / Verses

1. El a - mor es com - pren - si - vo. El a -
2. El a - mor nun - ca se_i - rri - ta. El a -
3. El a - mor dis - cul - pa to - do. El a -
1. *Love is kind and un - der - stand-ing In its*
2. *Not quick - tem - pered or re - sent - ful, Prone to*
3. *Love is quick to be for - giv - ing. Spread-ing*

mor es ser - vi - cial. El a - mor no tie - ne_en -
mor no_es des - cor - tés. El a - mor no_es e - go -
mor es ca - ri - dad. No se_a - le - gra de lo_in -
words and in its deeds, Nev - er pomp-ous, nev - er
take of - fense or brood: Love is pa - tient and un -
love is love's de - light. Love does not re - joice at

D.C.

vi - dia. El a - mor no bus - ca_el mal.
ís - ta. El a - mor nun - ca_es do - blez.
jus - to. Só - lo go - za_en la ver - dad.
jeal - ous, But at - tuned to oth - ers' needs.
self - ish, Nev - er boast-ful, nev - er rude.
e - vil, But re - joic - es in the right.

4. El amor soporta todo.
   El amor todo lo cree.
   El amor todo lo espera.
   El amor es siempre fiel.

5. Nuestra fe, nuestra esperanza,
   Frente a Dios terminará.
   El amor es algo eterno.
   Nunca, nunca pasará.

4. Bearing all, believing all things,
   Love endures and love prevails.
   Ever hopeful, ever faithful,
   By God's grace, love never fails.

5. All our faith and all our hoping
   God will bless and fortify.
   Love is holy and eternal
   And will never, never die.

Texto: Anónimo; tr. por Mary Louise Bringle, n.1953, © 2005, GIA Publications, Inc.
Música: Tradicional; arm. por Ronald F. Krisman, n.1946, © 2005, GIA Publications, Inc.

59 Cuán Gloriosa Será la Mañana
O How Glorious Shall Be That Great Morning

Estrofas / Verses

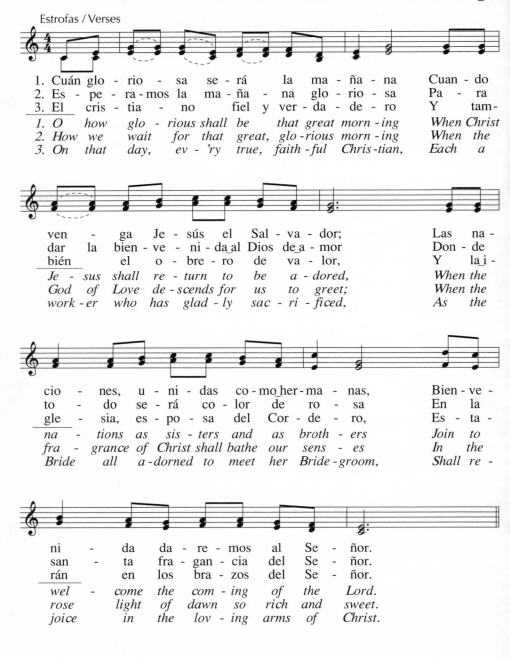

1. Cuán glo - rio - sa se - rá la ma - ña - na Cuan - do
2. Es - pe - ra - mos la ma - ña - na glo - rio - sa Pa - ra
3. El cris - tia - no fiel y ver - da - de - ro Y tam-

1. *O how glo - rious shall be that great morn - ing When Christ*
2. *How we wait for that great, glo - rious morn - ing When the*
3. *On that day, ev - 'ry true, faith - ful Chris - tian, Each a*

ven - ga Je - sús el Sal - va - dor; Las na -
dar la bien - ve - ni - da al Dios de a - mor Don - de
bién el o - bre - ro de va - lor, Y la i -

Je - sus shall re - turn to be a - dored, When the
God of Love de - scends for us to greet; When the
work - er who has glad - ly sac - ri - ficed, As the

cio - nes, u - ni - das co - mo her - ma - nas, Bien - ve -
to - do se - rá co - lor de ro - sa En la
gle - sia, es - po - sa del Cor - de - ro, Es - ta -

na - tions as sis - ters and as broth - ers Join to
fra - grance of Christ shall bathe our sens - es In the
Bride all a - dorned to meet her Bride - groom, Shall re -

ni - da da - re - mos al Se - ñor.
san - ta fra - gan - cia del Se - ñor.
rán en los bra - zos del Se - ñor.

wel - come the com - ing of the Lord.
rose light of dawn so rich and sweet.
joice in the lov - ing arms of Christ.

Estribillo / Refrain

No ha - brá ne - ce - si - dad de la luz el res - plan - dor,
For the bril - liance of that dawn shall out - shine the bright - est sun,

Ni el sol da - rá su luz, ni tam - po - co su ca - lor;
All its heat and light re - placed by the ra - diance of God's grace.

A - llí llan - to no ha - brá, ni tris - te - za, ni do - lor,
No more weep - ing shall re - main, no more grief and no more pain;

Por - que en - ton - ces Je - sús, el Rey del cie - lo,
For at last Je - sus Christ, the Lamb of heav - en

Pa - ra siem - pre se - rá Con - so - la - dor.
Throned in mer - cy, for - ev - er - more shall reign!

Texto: Felicia y Mariano Beltrán; tr. por Mary Louise Bringle, n.1953, © 2005, GIA Publications, Inc.
Música: Tradicional; arm. por Ronald F. Krisman, n.1946, © 2005, GIA Publications, Inc.

60 The Lord Is My Light
El Señor Es Mi Luz y Mi Salvación

Verse 1 / Estrofa 1

1. The Lord is my light and my sal - va - tion, the
1. El Se - ñor es mi luz y mi sal - va - ción, el Se -

Lord is my light and my sal - va - tion, the Lord is my
ñor es mi luz y mi sal - va - ción, el Se - ñor es mi

light and my sal - va - tion; whom shall I fear?
luz y mi sal - va - ción, ¿a quién te - me - ré?

Refrain / Estribillo

Whom shall I fear, whom shall I
¿A quién te - me - ré? ¿A quién te - me -

fear? ... The Lord is the strength
ré? ... El Se - ñor es la fuer - za

To verses

of my life; whom shall I fear?
de mi vi -da, ¿a quién te - me - ré?

Verse 2 / Estrofa 2

2. In the time of trou - ble he shall
2. El dí - a del pe - li - gro, Él me_es -con - de -

hide me, in the time of trou - ble, he shall
rá. El dí - a del pe - li - gro, Él me_es -con - de -

hide me, in the time of trou - ble, he shall
rá. El dí - a del pe - li - gro, Él me_es -con - de -

D.S.

Verse 3 / Estrofa 3

hide me; whom shall I fear?
rá. ¿A quién te - me - ré?

3. Wait on the Lord and be of good
3. Es - pe - ra en el Se - ñor y sé va -

cour - age, O wait on the Lord and be of good
lien - te, es - pe - ra en el Se - ñor y sé va -

cour - age, wait on the Lord and be of good
lien - te, es - pe - ra en el Se - ñor y sé va -

cour - age. He shall strength - en thine heart.
lien - te. Con - fí - a en el Se - ñor.

D.S.

Text: Psalm 27; Lillian Bouknight, © 1980, Savgos Music, Inc.; tr. by Ronald F. Krisman, b.1946, © 2005, GIA Publications, Inc.
Tune: Lillian Bouknight, arr. by Paul Gainer, © 1980, Savgos Music, Inc.

Somos Uno en Cristo / We Are All One in Christ   61

So-mos u-no en Cris-to, so-mos u-no. So-mos u-no,
We are all one in Christ, we are one bod-y, *all one peo-ple*

1. u-no so-lo.
2. so-lo. Un so-lo Dios, un so-lo Se-
out of man-y. *man-y. There is one God, and on-ly one*

ñor, u-na so-la fe, un so-lo_a-mor. Un so-lo bau-
Lord; there is one faith, one ho-ly love. There is one

tis-mo, un so-lo_Es-pí-ri-tu, y_e-se_es el Con-so-la-dor.
bap-tism; there is one Spir-it, who is God the com-fort-er.

Texto: Anónimo; tr. por Gerhard Cartford, n.1923, © 1998, Augsburg Fortress
Música: SOMOS UNO, Irregular; anónimo

62 Morning Has Broken / Despunta el Alba

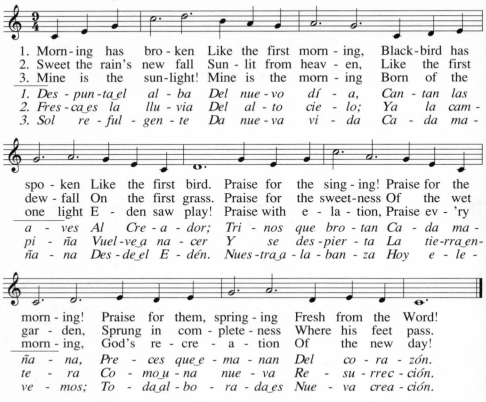

1. Morn-ing has bro-ken Like the first morn-ing, Black-bird has
2. Sweet the rain's new fall Sun-lit from heav-en, Like the first
3. Mine is the sun-light! Mine is the morn-ing Born of the

1. Des-pun-ta_el al-ba Del nue-vo dí-a, Can-tan las
2. Fres-ca_es la llu-via Del al-to cie-lo; Ya la cam-
3. Sol re-ful-gen-te Da nue-va vi-da Ca-da ma-

spo-ken Like the first bird. Praise for the sing-ing! Praise for the
dew-fall On the first grass. Praise for the sweet-ness Of the wet
one light E-den saw play! Praise with e-la-tion, Praise ev-'ry

a-ves Al Cre-a-dor; Tri-nos que bro-tan Ca-da ma-
pi-ña Vuel-ve_a na-cer Y se des-pier-ta La tie-rra_en-
ña-na Des-de_el E-dén. Nues-tra_a-la-ban-za Hoy e-le-

morn-ing! Praise for them, spring-ing Fresh from the Word!
gar-den, Sprung in com-plete-ness Where his feet pass.
morn-ing, God's re-cre-a-tion Of the new day!

ña-na, Pre-ces que_e-ma-nan Del co-ra-zón.
te-ra Co-mo_u-na nue-va Re-su-rrec-ción.
ve-mos; To-da_al-bo-ra-da_es Nue-va crea-ción.

Text: Eleanor Farjeon, 1881-1965, *The Children's Bells*, © David Higham Assoc., Ltd.; tr. by the editorial committee of *Albricias*,
   © 1987, Comisión de "Albricias." Used with permission.
Music: BUNESSAN, 5 5 5 4 D; Scots Gaelic; acc. by Robert J. Batastini, b.1942, © 1999, GIA Publications, Inc.

63 They'll Know We Are Christians
Somos Uno en Espíritu

1. We are one in the Spir-it, we are
2. We will walk with each oth-er, we will
3. We will work with each oth-er, we will
4. All praise to the Fa-ther, from

1. So-mos u-no_en es-pí-ri-tu y_en
2. Mar-cha-re-mos to ma-dos de la
3. Tra-ba-je-mos u-ni-dos la-do_a
4. Glo-ria_al Pa-dre que_es fuen-te de

one   in   the   Lord,   We   are   one   in   the
walk   hand in   hand,   We   will   walk   with each
work   side by   side,   We   will   work   with each
whom   all   things come,   And   all   praise to   Christ
el   *Se* -   *ñor;* *So* *mos* *u*   *no_en* *es*-
ma -   *no_en a* -   *mor,* *Mar* *cha* - *re* - *mos* *to* -
la -   *do_en a* -   *mor,* *Tra* *ba* - *je* - *mos* *u*-
to - *da*   *ben* - *di* - *ción;* *Glo* - *ria_a* *Cris* - *to* *su*

Spir - it,   we   are   one   in   the   Lord,   And   we
oth - er,   we   will   walk   hand in   hand,   And   to -
oth - er,   we   will   work   side by   side,   And   we'll
Je - sus,   his   on - ly   Son,   And   all
pí - *ri* - *tu*   *y_en* *el*   *Se* -   *ñor*   *Y*   *ro*-
ma - *dos* *de*   *la*   *ma* - *no_en a* - *mor,* *A* - *nun*-
ni - *dos* *la* - *do_a* *la* - *do_en a* - *mor,* *Co* - *mo*
Hi - *jo*   *que* *nos* *da*   *la* *sal* - *va* - *ción* *Y_al* *Es*-

pray   that   all   u - ni - ty   may   one   day   be   re - stored:
geth - er we'll spread the   news that   God   is   in   our   land:
guard   hu - man's dig - ni - ty and   save hu - man's pride:
praise   to   the   Spir - it,   who   makes us   one:
ga -   *mos que_un dí* - *a*   *nues-tra_u-nión* *se* - *a*   *to* - *tal.*
cian - *do que_en es* - *ta*   *tie* - *rra* *vi* - *ve* *y_o* - *bra* *Dios.*
guar - *das* *ce* - *lo* - *sos* *de* *la* *gen* - *te* *en* *su_ho* - *nor.*
pí - *ri* - *tu*   *San* - *to* *que* *nos* *u* - *ne_en* *co* - *mu* - *nión.*

And   they'll know   we   are   Chris - tians by   our   love,   by   our
Y   *que*   *so* - *mos cris* - *tia* - *nos* *lo* *sa* - *brán,* *lo* *sa*-

love, Yes, they'll know   we   are   Chris - tians by   our   love.
brán, Por - *que_u* - *ni* - *dos* *es* - *ta* - *mos* *en*   *a* - *mor.*

Text: Peter Scholtes, b.1938; tr. by Federico J. Pagura, b.1923, alt.
Tune: ST. BRENDAN'S, 7 6 7 6 8 6 with refrain; Peter Scholtes, b.1938
© 1966, F.E.L. Publications, assigned to The Lorenz Corp., 1991

64   Blest Are They / Benditos los Pobres

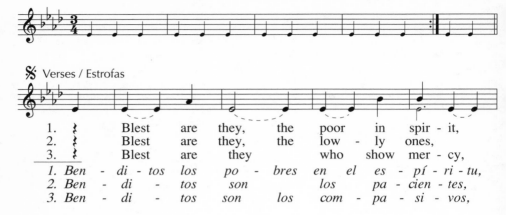

Verses / Estrofas

1.	Blest	are	they,	the	poor	in	spir - it,
2.	Blest	are	they,	the	low - ly	ones,
3.	Blest	are	they		who	show	mer - cy,
1. Ben - di - tos	los	po - bres	en	el	es - pí - ri - tu,
2. Ben - di - tos	son		los	pa - cien - tes,
3. Ben - di - tos	son	los	com - pa - si - vos,

theirs	is	the	king - dom	of	God.
they	shall	in - her - it	the	earth.
mer - cy	shall	be	theirs.
su - yo_es	el	rei - no	de	Dios.	Di -
he - re - da - rán	la	tie - rra.	Di -
ob - ten - drán	pie - dad.	Di -

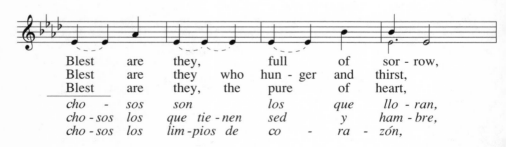

Blest	are	they,	full	of	sor - row,
Blest	are	they who	hun - ger	and	thirst,
Blest	are	they, the	pure	of	heart,
cho - sos	son	los	que	llo - ran,
cho - sos	los	que tie - nen	sed	y	ham - bre,
cho - sos	los	lim - pios de	co - ra - zón,

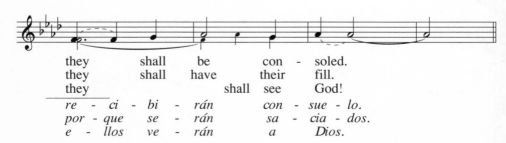

they	shall	be	con - soled.
they	shall	have	their	fill.
they		shall	see	God!
re - ci - bi - rán	con - sue - lo.
por - que	se - rán	sa - cia - dos.
e - llos	ve - rán	a	Dios.

Refrain / Estribillo

Descant:

Re - joice and be glad!
¡A - lé - gren -se y con - tén - ten - se!

Melody:

Re - joice and be glad!
¡A - lé - gren -se y con - tén - ten - se!

Men's voices:

Re - joice and be glad!
¡A - le - gres con - tén - ten - se!

Bless-ed are you, ho - ly are you! Re - joice
¡Son los ben - di - tos de nues-tro Dios! ¡A - lé-gren -se

Bless-ed are you, ho - ly are you! Re - joice
¡Son los ben - di - tos de nues-tro Dios! ¡A - lé-gren -se

Bless-ed, ho - ly are you! Re -
¡Son ben - di -tos por Dios! ¡A -

and be glad! Yours is the king-dom of
y con - tén -ten - se! ¡Su - yo_es el rei - no de

and be glad! Yours is the king-dom of
y con - tén -ten - se! ¡Su - yo_es el rei - no de

joice and be glad! Yours is the king-dom of
le - gres con -tén -ten - se! ¡Su - yo_es el rei - no de

1.-4.   To verses || Last time

God!   God!
Dios!   *Dios!*

God!   God!
Dios!   *Dios!*

God!   God!
Dios!   *Dios!*

Verses 4, 5 / Estrofas 4, 5

4. ≀ Blest are they who seek peace;
5. ≀ Blest are you who suf - fer hate,
4. Ben - di - tos los que por la paz tra - ba - jan,
5. Ben - di - tos son los per - se - gui - dos,

they are the chil - dren of God.
all be - cause of me. Re -
e - llos son hi - jos de Dios. Di -
to - do por cau - sa mi - a. ¡A -

Blest are they who suf - fer in faith, the
joice and be glad, yours is the king - dom;
cho - sos los que por la fe su - fren,
lé - gren - se! Su re - com - pen - sa

To refrain

glo - ry of God is theirs.
shine for all to see.
su - ya_es la glo - ria de Dios.
gran - de_en el cie - lo se - rá.

Text: Matthew 5:3-12; David Haas, b.1957, tr. by Ronald F. Krisman, b.1946
Tune: David Haas, b.1957; vocal arr. by David Haas and Michael Joncas, b.1951
© 1985, 2005, GIA Publications, Inc.

Cantad al Señor / Sing Praise to the Lord   65

1. Can - tad al Se - ñor un cán - ti - co nue - vo.
2. Él es Cre - a - dor y due - ño de to - do.
3. Can - tad a Je - sús, por - que Él es dig - no.
1. *Sing praise to the Lord, O sing out a new song.*
2. *Cre - a - tor of all, God rules with com - pas - sion.*
3. *Ac - claim Je - sus Christ as wor - thy of hon - or.*

Can - tad al Se - ñor un cán - ti - co nue - vo.
Él es Cre - a - dor y due - ño de to - do.
Can - tad a Je - sús, por - que Él es dig - no.
Sing praise to the Lord, O sing out a new song.
Cre - a - tor of all, God rules with com - pas - sion.
Ac - claim Je - sus Christ as wor - thy of hon - or.

Can - tad al Se - ñor un cán - ti - co nue - vo.
Él es Cre - a - dor y due - ño de to - do.
Can - tad a Je - sús, por - que Él es dig - no.
Sing praise to the Lord, O sing out a new song.
Cre - a - tor of all, God rules with com - pas - sion.
Ac - claim Je - sus Christ as wor - thy of hon - or.

¡Can - tad al Se - ñor, Can - tad al Se - ñor!
Sing praise to the Lord, Sing praise to our God.

4. Es Él quien nos da su Espíritu Santo. . .
   ¡Cantad al Señor, cantad al Señor!

5. Cantad al Señor: "¡Amén, aleluya!". . .
   ¡Cantad al Señor, cantad al Señor!

4. Give thanks to the Lord,
   who sends us the Spirit. . .
   Sing praise to the Lord,
   Sing praise to our God.

5. Sing praise to the Lord,
   "Amen, Alleluia!". . .
   Sing praise to the Lord,
   Sing praise to our God.

Texto: Anónimo, alt., Tradicional de Brasil; tr. por Ronald F. Krisman, n.1946, © 2005, GIA Publications, Inc.
Música: CANTAI AO SENHOR, 11 11 11 10; Tradicional de Brasil; arm. por Ronald F. Krisman, n.1946, © 2005, GIA Publications, Inc.

66 You Are Mine / Contigo Estoy

Verses / Estrofas

1. I will come to you in the si - lence,
2. I am hope for all who are hope - less,
3. I am strength for all the de - spair - ing,
4. am the Word that leads all to free - dom,   I

1. Te ha - bla - ré en la paz del si - len - cio,
2. es - pe - ran - za de quien an - he - la,   la
3. Soy la for - ta - le - za del dé - bil;
4. Soy pa - la - bra li - be - ra - do - ra,   la

I will lift you from all your fear.
I am eyes for all who long to see.   In the
heal - ing for the ones who dwell in shame.
am the peace the world can - not give.

y del mie - do te li - bra - ré.   ⁊ Mi
vis - ta de los que no pue - den ver.   ⁊ Los
al a - ver - gon - za - do e - xal - ta - ré.   ⁊ Tu
paz que el mun - do no pue - de dar.

You will hear my voice, I claim you as my choice, be
shad - ows of the night, I will be your light,
All the blind will see, the lame will all run free, and
I will call your name, em - brac - ing all your pain. Stand

voz es - cu - cha - rás, y mí - o tú se - rás,
Con in - ten - si - dad bri - lla - ré en la os-cu - ri - dad.
cie - gos ve - rán, los li - sia - dos co - rre - rán.   Mi
nom - bre lla - ma - ré; tu llan - to to - ma - ré.   Le -

still and know I am here. (To verse 2)
come and rest in me. (To refrain)
all will know my name. (To refrain)
up, now walk, and live! (To refrain)

Jun - to a ti es - ta - ré. (A la Estrofa 2)
Tu des-can - so quie - ro ser. (Al Estribillo)   2. Soy
nom - bre re - ve - la - ré. (Al Estribillo)
ván - ta - te a ca - mi - nar. (Al Estribillo)

Refrain / Estribillo

Do not be a-fraid, I am with you. I have called you each by
A-quí es-toy con-ti - go, no te - mas. *Yo por nom-bre te lla -*

name. Come and fol - low me, I will bring you
mé. *Ven y sí - gue -me.* *Yo te lle -va -*

home; I love you and you are mine.
ré. *Te a - mo y con-ti - go es - toy.*

D.C. | Final ending

4. I

Text: David Haas, b.1957; tr. by Santiago Fernández, b.1971
Tune: David Haas, b.1957
© 1991, 2005, GIA Publications, Inc.

67 De Colores / Sing of Colors

1. De co - lo - res, de co - lo - res se vis - ten los
2. De co - lo - res, de co - lo - res bri - llan - tes y
3. Ju - bi - lo - sos, ju - bi - lo - sos vi - va - mos en
4. Can - ta el ga - llo, can-ta el ga - llo con el qui - ri,
1. *Sing of col -ors, sing of col - ors that o - ver the*
2. *Sing, re -joic-ing! Ev - 'ry crea-ture that breathes, raise a*

cam - pos en la pri - ma - ve - ra. De co -
fi - nos se vis - te la au - ro - ra. De co -
gra - cia pues - to que se pue - de. Sa - cia -
qui - ri, qui - ri, qui - ri, qui - ri; La ga -
hills in pro - fu - sion are spring - ing. Sing of
song to the God of cre - a - tion. Sing, re -

lo - res, de co - lo - res son los pa - ja - ri - tos que
lo - res, de co - lo - res son los mil re - fle - jos que el
re - mos, sa - cia - re - mos la sed ar - do - ro - sa del
lli - na, la ga - lli - na con el ca - ra, ca - ra, ca -
col - ors of the birds that fly out -side my win - dow, their
joic - ing! Sing to God who so ear -nest - ly cares, who has

vie - nen de a - fue - ra. De co - lo - res, de co -
sol a - te - so - ra. De co - lo - res, de co -
Rey que no mue - re. Ju - bi - lo - sos, ju - bi -
ra, ca - ra, ca - ra; Los po - llue - los, los po -
can - ti - cles sing -ing. Sing of col - ors, in the
of - fered sal - va - tion. Sing the good news! Sing the

lo - res   es   el ar - co   i - ris   que ve - mos   sa - lir,
lo - res   se   vis-te_el dia - man - te   que ve - mos   lu - cir,
lo - sos   lle - ve - mos   a   Cris - to   un   al - ma_y mil   más,
llue - los   con   el   pí - o,   pí - o,   pí - o,   pí - o,   pí.
rain - bow's bright col - ors God's prom - ise   of hope we   re - call.
love   of   the   Sav - ior   re - flect - ing   the   col - ors   of   all.

Y   por   e - so   los gran - des   a - mo - res   de   mu - chos co -
Y   por   e - so   los gran - des   a - mo - res   de   mu - chos co -
Di - fun - dien - do   la   luz que_i - lu - mi - na   la   gra - cia di -
Y   por   e - so   los gran - des   a - mo - res   de   mu - chos co -
Sing of   col - ors that make   up   the   earth, and give thanks to   the
Man - y   col - ors that shine from God's face, man - y   col - ors that

lo - res me gus-tan a   mí,   Y   por   e - so   los   gran - des   a -
lo - res me gus-tan a   mí,   Y   por   e - so   los   gran - des   a -
vi - na   del gran i - de - al,   Di - fun - dien - do   la   luz que_i - lu -
lo - res me gus-tan a   mí,   Y   por   e - so   los   gran - des   a -
God who cre - at - ed us   all.   Sing of   col - ors that make   up   the
tell   us God's love to   re - call.   Man - y   col - ors that shine from God's

mo - res   de   mu - chos co - lo - res   me   gus - tan a   mí.
mo - res   de   mu - chos co - lo - res   me   gus - tan a   mí.
mi - na   la   gra - cia di - vi - na   del gran i - de - al.
mo - res   de   mu - chos co - lo - res   me   gus - tan a   mí.
earth, and give thanks to   the   God who cre - at - ed us   all.
face, man - y   col - ors that tell   us God's love to   re - call.

Texto: Tradicional; tr. por *The New Century Hymnal,* © 1995, Pilgrim Press
Música: Tradicional; arm. por Ronald F. Krisman, n.1946, © 2005, GIA Publications, Inc.

68   I Say "Yes," Lord / Digo "Sí," Señor

Verses

Cantor:

1. To the God who can-not die:
   To the God of the op-pressed:
2. I am a ser-vant of the Lord:
   I'm a pris-oner of their wars:
3. For the dream I have to-day:
   To come to love my en-e-mies:
4. Like that of Job, un-ceas-ing-ly:
   Like that of Da-vid in a song:

I say
Di-go

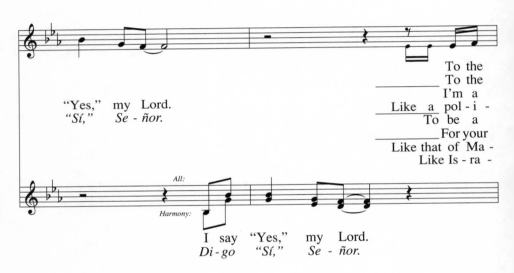

"Yes," my Lord.
"Sí," Se-ñor.

To the
To the
I'm a
Like a pol-i-
To be a
For your
Like that of Ma-
Like Is-ra-

All:

Harmony:

I say "Yes," my Lord.
Di-go "Sí," Se-ñor.

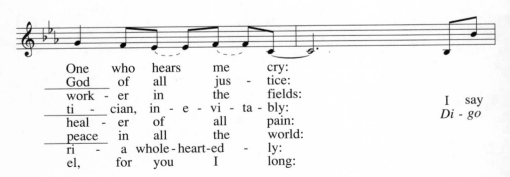

One who hears me cry:
God of all jus-tice:
work-er in the fields:
ti-cian, in-e-vi-ta-bly:
heal-er of all pain:
peace in all the world:
ri-a whole-heart-ed-ly:
el, for you I long:

I say
Di-go

"Yes," my Lord.
"Sí," Se - ñor.

All:

Harmony:

I say "Yes," my Lord.　"Yes," my Lord.
Di - go "Sí," Se - ñor.　"Sí," Se - ñor.

Refrain / Estribillo

Descant:

I　say　"Yes," my Lord,　in　all　the　good　times, through
Di - go　"Sí," Se - ñor,　en　tiem - pos ma - los,　en

Melody:

I　say　"Yes," my Lord,　in　all　the　good　times, through
Di - go　"Sí," Se - ñor,　en　tiem - pos ma - los,　en

all　the　bad　times,　I　say　"Yes," my Lord,　to
tiem - pos bue - nos,　Di - go　"Sí," Se - ñor,　a

all　the　bad　times,　I　say　"Yes," my Lord,　to
tiem - pos bue - nos,　Di - go　"Sí," Se - ñor,　a

Last time to coda ⊕　　　**D.C.** ⊕ **Coda**

ev - 'ry　word　you　speak.
to - do　lo　que_ha - blas.

ev - 'ry　word　you　speak.
to - do　lo　que_ha - blas.

Estrofas

Cantor:

1. Al Se - ñor de e - ter - ni - dad,
   Al Dios de los o - pri - mi - dos,
2. Soy un sir - vien - te del Se - ñor,
   Co - mo un pri - sio - ne - ro de gue - rra, Di - go
3. Por el sue - ño que ten - go hoy,
   Pa - ra a - mar a mis e - ne - mi - gos,
4. Co - mo Job in - ce - san - ta - men - te,
   Co - mo Da - vid en u - na can - ción,

"Sí," Se - ñor.   Al Se -
                                                     Al
                                                     Y tra -
Co - mo un po -
Pa - ra sa -
Y por la
Co - mo Ma -
Co - mo Is - ra -

ñor   que   me_es - cu - cha,
Dios   de   jus - ti - cia,
ba - jo   en   los   cam - pos,
lí - ti - co in - e - vi - ta - ble,   Di - go
nar a   los que_es - tán su - frien - do,
paz en   los   go - bier - nos,
rí - a   com - ple - ta - men - te,
el   lle - no de_es - pe - ran - za,

1.   2.

"Sí," Se - ñor.

Text: Donna Peña, b.1955
Tune: Donna Peña, b.1955; arr. by Marty Haugen, b.1950
© 1989, GIA Publications, Inc.

Eye Has Not Seen / Ni Ojo Ni Oído   69

Refrain / Estribillo

Eye has not seen, ear has not heard what
Ni o - jo ni o - í - do pue - de sa - ber lo que

God has read-y for those who love him;
Dios ha pre-pa - ra-do pa-ra los que lo a-man.

Spir - it of love, come, give us the mind of
Ven, San-to Es - pí - ri - tu, haz-nos pen - sar cual

Last time

Je - sus, teach us the wis-dom of God.
Cris - to y ver los mis - te - rios de Dios.

Last time

Verses 1-3 / Estrofas 1-3

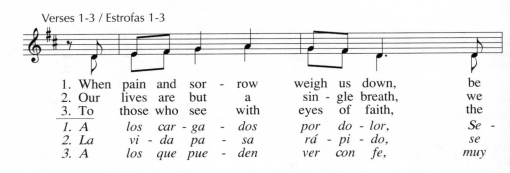

1. When pain and sor - row weigh us down, be
2. Our lives are but a sin - gle breath, we
3. To those who see with eyes of faith, the

1. A los car - ga - dos por do - lor, Se -
2. La vi - da pa - sa rá - pi - do, se
3. A los que pue - den ver con fe, muy

near to us, O Lord, for - give the weak - ness
flow - er and we fade, yet all our days are
Lord is ev - er near, re - flect - ed in the

ñor, tú cer - ca_es - tás per - do - na nues - tra
se - ca co - mo flor; mas nues - tros dí - as,
cer - ca_es - tás, Se - ñor, te ve - mos en los

of our faith, and bear us up with - in your peace - ful
in your hands, so we re - turn in love what love has
fac - es of all the poor and low - ly of the

dé - bil fe, y há - bla - nos pa - la - bras de tu
tu - yos son: te da - mos lo que_has he - cho en tu_a -
po - bres y_hu - mil - des: les da - mos nues - tro_a -

D.C.

word.
made.
world.

paz.
mor.
mor.

Verse 4 / Estrofa 4

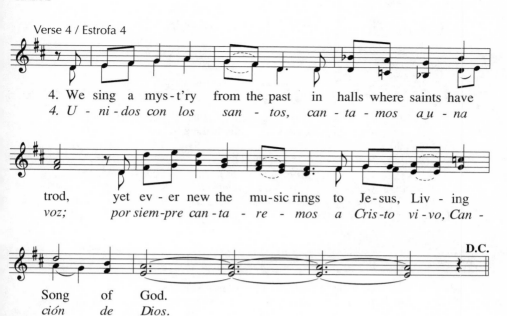

4. We sing a mys-t'ry from the past in halls where saints have
4. U - ni -dos con los san - tos, can -ta -mos a u - na

trod, yet ev - er new the mu-sic rings to Je - sus, Liv - ing
voz; por siem-pre can -ta - re - mos a Cris-to vi -vo, Can -

D.C.

Song of God.
ción de Dios.

Text: 1 Corinthians 2:9-10; Marty Haugen, b.1950; tr. by Ronald F. Krisman, b.1946
Tune: Marty Haugen, b.1950
© 1982, 2005, GIA Publications, Inc.

70   Canto de Alegría / Joyfully We Sing Here

Estrofas / Verses

1. Can - to de_a - le - grí - a   por - que   ten - go_a - mor.
2. Del   a - mor   de   Cris - to,   ¿quién me_a - par - ta - rá?
3. To - do   lo   que   pa - sa   en   mi   vi - da_a - quí
4. En   las prue - bas   to - das Dios   a - yu - da - rá.

1. Joy - ful - ly   we   sing here   of   the   Sav - ior's grace,
2. Who can sep - a - rate   us   from   the   love   of   Christ?
3. Ev - 'ry-thing that   hap - pens   to   us   day   by   day,
4. God re -mains our   ref - uge   in   the   trials   we   face,

Vi - vo ca - da   dí - a   con   el   Sal - va - dor.
Es - con - di - do_en Cris - to, ¿quién me   to - ca - rá?
Dios   me   lo   pre - pa - ra   pa - ra   bien   de mí.
No   nos des - am - pa - ra,   no   nos   de - ja - rá.

Liv - ing   ev - 'ry   day   with - in   his   warm em - brace.
Who,   pre - vail   a - gainst, when God   is   on   our side?
Christ will   be   the   bea - con   who   will   light   our way.
Shield -ing   and   sus - tain - ing   us   with   lov - ing grace.

Quie - ro_a   to - do_el mun - do   de   Él   siem - pre_ha - blar,
Si   Dios   jus - ti - fi - ca, ¿quién con - de - na - rá?
En   mis prue - bas   du - ras, Dios me_es siem - pre   fiel:
Él   nos   ne - ce - si - ta   pa - ra   tra - ba - jar.

Ea - ger - ly   we   long, both now   and   ev - 'ry - where,
In - ter - ced - ing   for   us, Christ   is   strong   and   sure.
Through dis - tress   and   per - il,   God   is   faith - ful   still.
Work - ing through the   la - bors   of   our hearts   and   hands,

Por - que   Cris - to   quie - re_a   to - dos   ya   sal - var.
Cris - to   por   mí_a - bo - ga, ¿quién me_a - cu - sa - rá?
¿Por   qué   pues   las   du - das?   Yo   des - can - so_en él.
Va - mos   a - de - lan - te,   va - mos   a   triun - far.

All   through -out   the   world, God's   sav - ing   love   to   share.
More   than   con -querors through him,   we   can   rest   se - cure.
Why should   we   be   anx - ious   if   we   trust God's will?
Christ will   lead   us   on - ward   in   tri - um - phant bands!

Estribillo / Refrain

Can - to   por-que ten - go a-mor.   Vi - vo
Sing - ing   of the Sav - ior's grace,   Liv - ing

con el Sal - va - dor.   Quie - ro   de Él
in his warm em - brace,   Long - ing,   now and

siem - pre ha - blar.   Cris - to   quie-re ya sal - var.
ev - 'ry - where,   All God's   sav-ing love to share.

Texto: Estrofas 1, 4, anónimo; estrofas 2, 3, Enrique S. Turrall, 1867-1953, alt.; tr. por Mary Louise Bringle, n.1953, © 2005, GIA Publications, Inc.
Música: ARGENTINA, 11 11 11 11 con estribillo; anónimo; arm. por Ronald F. Krisman, n.1946, © 2005, GIA Publications, Inc.

71 We Are Many Parts / Muchos Miembros Hay

Refrain / Estribillo

We are man-y parts, we are all one
Mu-chos miem-bros hay, en un so-lo

bod-y, and the gifts we have we are giv-en to
cuer-po; nues-tros do-nes son pa-ra dar y ser-

share. May the Spir-it of love
vir. Que_el Es-pí-ri-tu de Dios

make us one in-deed; one, the love that we
nos u-na en su_a-mor; com-par-tien-do_el do-

share, one, our hope in de - spair,
lor, *com - ba - tien - do el te - mor,*

one, the cross that we bear.
com - pla - cien - do al Se - ñor.

Last time

Last time

Verses / Estrofas
unis.

1. God of all, we look to you, we would be your
2. So my pain is pain for you, in your joy is
3. All you seek - ers, great and small, seek the great - est
1. *Oh Se - ñor, que - re - mos ser ser - vi - do - res*
2. *Mi do - lor te due - le a tí; si te go - zas,*
3. *Quie - nes bus - can de ver - dad su ma - yor fe -*

div.
D.C.

ser - vants true, let us be your love to all the world.
my joy, too; all is brought to - geth - er in the Lord.
gift of all; if you love, then you will know the Lord.
por do - quier; y a la hu - ma - ni - dad lle - var tu a - mor.
soy fe - liz; to - do se u - ne en tor - no al Se - ñor.
li - ci - dad: a - men y co - no - ce - rán a Dios.

div.

Text: 1 Corinthians 12, 13; Marty Haugen, b.1950; tr. by Santiago Fernández, b.1971
Tune: Marty Haugen, b.1950
© 1980, 1986, 2005, GIA Publications, Inc.

72 Dios Es Amor / Glory and Praise, Alleluia

Estribillo / Refrain

Dios es a - mor, a - le - lu - ya; vi - va_el a - mor.
Glo - ry and praise, al - le - lu - ia, for God is love.

¡A - le - lu - ya!
Al - le - lu - ia!

Can - te - mos muy a -
Sing out with joy and

le - gres es - ta can - ción, can - ción de_a - mor.
glad - ness this song of love. Al - le - lu - ia!

Estrofas / Verses

1. Ben - de - cid al Se - ñor, pue - blos to - dos,
2. Que la llu - via y_el vien - to le cla - men,
3. Bru - mas, nie - ve, y_es - car - cha le can - ten,

1. *Bless the Lord, all you na - tions and peo - ples,*
2. *Praise your God, dew and rain, winds and breez - es,*
3. *Ice and snow, frost and chill, bless your Mak - er,*

¡A - le - lu - ya! ¡A - le - lu - ya!
Al - le - lu - ia! Al - le - lu - ia!

A - cla - mad - le y can - tad - le por siem - pre.
No - che_y dí - a su nom - bre pro - cla - men.
Hu - ra - ca - nes, tor - men - tas lo_a - la - ben.

Of - fer God ac - cla - ma - tions un - ceas - ing.
Nights and days, light and dark - ness, sing prais - es.
Make an awe - some dis - play, storms and light - ning.

¡A - le - lu - ya!   ¡A - le - lu - ya!
Al - le - lu - ia!   *Al - le - lu - ia!*

4. Tierra entera
y cuanto existe, ¡Aleluya!
Proclamemos por siempre
su nombre. ¡Aleluya!

5. Gloria demos al
Padre y al Hijo, ¡Aleluya!
Y al Espíritu Santo
por siempre. ¡Aleluya!

4. Ev'ry creature on earth,
shout God's praises, Alleluia!
Blest be God's holy
name for all ages. Alleluia!

5. Glory be to our
wondrous Creator, Alleluia!
Praised be Christ and the
Spirit for ever, Alleluia!

Texto: Daniel 3:56-88; Carlos Rosas, n.1939, © 1976, Resource Publications. Derechos reservados. Con las debidas licencias; tr. por Ronald F. Krisman, n.1946, © 2005, GIA Publications, Inc.
Música: Carlos Rosas, n.1939, © 1976, Resource Publications. Derechos reservados. Con las debidas licencias; arm. por Ronald F. Krisman, n.1946, © 2005, GIA Publications, Inc.

73 How Great Thou Art / Señor, Mi Dios

1. O Lord my God, when I in awe-some
2. When thru the woods and for-est glades I
3. And when I think that God, His Son not

1. Se - ñor, mi Dios, al con - tem - plar los
2. Al re - co - rrer los mon - tes y los
3. Cuan - do me_a - cuer - do de tu_a - mor di -

won - der Con - sid - er all the worlds Thy hands have
wan - der And hear the birds sing sweet - ly in the
spar - ing, Sent Him to die, I scarce can take it

cie - los, El fir - ma - men - to_y las es - tre - llas
va - lles Y ver las be - llas flo - res al pa -
vi - no Que des-de_el cie - lo_al Sal - va - dor en -

made, I see the stars, I hear the roll - ing
trees, When I look down from loft - y moun-tain
in That on the cross, my bur - den glad - ly

mil, Al o - ir tu voz en los po - ten - tes
sar, Al es - cu - char el can - to de las
vió, A - quel Je - sús, que por sal - var - me

thun - der, Thy pow'r thru - out the un - i - verse dis - played!
gran - deur And hear the brook and feel the gen - tle breeze.
bear - ing, He bled and died to take a - way my sin!
true - nos Y ver bri - llar el sol en su ce - nit,
a - ves Y el mur - mu - rar del cla - ro ma - nan - tial,
vi - no Y en u - na cruz por mí su - frió y mu - rió,

Then sings my soul, my Sav - ior God, to Thee; How great Thou
Mi co - ra - zón en - to - na la can - ción. ¡Cuán gran - de

art, how great Thou art! Then sings my soul, my Sav - ior God, to
e - res, oh Se - ñor! Mi co - ra - zón en - to - na la can-

Thee; How great Thou art, How great Thou art!
ción. ¡Cuán gran - de e - res, oh Se - ñor!

4. When Christ shall come
   with shout of acclamation
And take me home,
   what joy shall fill my heart!
Then I shall bow
   in humble adoration
And there proclaim, my God,
   how great Thou art!

4. Cuando me lleves,
   Dios, a tu presencia,
Al dulce hogar,
   al cielo de esplendor;
Te adoraré,
   cantando la grandeza
De tu poder
   y tu infinito amor.

Text: Stuart K. Hine, 1899-1989; Spanish tr. by Arturo W. Hotton Rives, 1909-1959, alt.
Tune: Stuart K. Hine, 1899-1989

74 Vamos Todos al Banquete
Let Us Go Now to the Banquet

Estribillo / Refrain

Va - mos   to - dos   al ban - que - te,   A la
Let us   go   now   to the ban - quet,   To the

me - sa de la   cre-a - ción;   Ca - da cual, con su ta - bu-
feast of the u - ni - verse.   The ta-ble's set and a place is

re - te,   Tie-ne un pues - to y u - na   mi - sión.
wait - ing; Come, ev - 'ry - one, with your gifts to share.

Estrofas / Verses

1. Hoy me   le - van - to muy   tem - pra - no,   Ya me es-
2. Dios in - vi - ta a   to - dos   los   po - bres   A es - ta
3. Dios nos man - da a ha - cer de es - te   mun - do   U - na

1. *I   will rise   in   the ear - ly   morn - ing.   The com-*
2. *God in - vites   all   the poor   and   hun - gry   To the*
3. *May we build   such   a place   a - mong   us   Where all*

pe - ra la co - mu - ni - dad.   Voy su-
me - sa co - mún   por la   fe,   Don - de
me - sa don-de ha - ya i-gual - dad;   Tra - ba-

mu - ni - ty's wait - ing for me.   With a
ban - quet of jus - tice and good,   Where the
peo - ple are e - qual in love.   God has

bien	-	do	a	-	le	-	gre	la	cues	-	ta,	Voy	en
no hay		a	-	ca	-	pa	-	ra	-	do	-	res	Don - de
jan	-	do y	lu	-	chan	-	do	jun	-	tos,	Com - par -
spring		*in*	*my*	*step*		*I'm*	*walk*	-	*ing*		*With*	*my*
har	-	*vest*	*will*	*not*		*be*	*hoard*	-	*ed,*		*So*	*that*
called		*us*	*to*	*work*		*to*	-	*geth*	-	*er*		*And*	*to*

D.C.

bus	-	ca	de	tu a	-	mis	-	tad.
to	-	dos	pue -	dan		co	-	mer.
tien	-	do	la	pro	-	pie	-	dad.
friends		*and*	*my*	*fam*	-	*i*	-	*ly.*
no		*one*	*will*	*lack*		*for*		*food.*
share		*ev* -	*'ry* - *thing*			*we*		*have.*

Texto: *Misa Popular Salvadoreña,* Guillermo Cuéllar; tr. por Bret Hesla y William Dexheimer-Pharris
Música: Guillermo Cuéllar; arm. por Ronald F. Krisman, n.1946
© 1994, 2005, GIA Publications, Inc.

75   Eat This Bread / Coman de Este Pan

Refrain / Estribillo

Eat this bread, drink this cup,
Je - sus Christ, bread of life,
Co - man de es - te pan, be - ban de es - te cá - liz,

come to him and nev - er be hun - gry.
those who come to you will not hun - ger.
ven - gan, y no ten - drán ham - bre.

Eat this bread, drink this cup,
Je - sus Christ, Ri - sen Lord,
Co - man de es - te pan, be - ban de es - te cá - liz,

trust in him and you will not thirst.
those who trust in you will not thirst.
cre - an, y no ten - drán sed.

Verses

Cantor:

D.C.

1. Christ is the bread of life, the true bread sent from the Fa - ther.

2. Our an-ces-tors ate man-na in the des-ert, but

this is the bread come down from heav-en. **D.C.**

3. Eat his flesh and drink his blood, and

Christ will raise you up on the last day. **D.C.**

4. An-y-one who eats this bread, will live for ev-er. **D.C.**

5. If we be-lieve and eat this bread, we will have e-ter-nal life. **D.C.**

Estrofas

Cantor:

1. *Cris-to es el Pan de Vi-da, el pan ver-da-de-ro del Pa-dre.* **D.C.**

2. *Co-mió Is-rael ma-ná en el de-sier-to, pe-ro es-te pan ba-jó del cie-lo.* **D.C.**

3. *To-men su Cuer-po y su San-gre, y Cris-to los re-su-ci-ta-rá.* **D.C.**

4. *Los que co-men es-te pan, vi-vi-rán por siem-pre.* **D.C.**

5. *Cre-an y co-man es-te pan, y ten-drán la vi-da e-ter-na.* **D.C.**

Text: John 6; adapt. by Robert J. Batastini, b.1942, and the Taizé Community; tr. by Ronald F. Krisman, b.1946
Tune: Jacques Berthier, 1923-1994
© 1984, 2005, Les Presses de Taizé, GIA Publications, Inc., agent

76 Arriba los Corazones / We Lift Up Our Hearts

Estribillo / Refrain

A - rri - ba los co - ra - zo - nes, Va - ya - mos to -
We lift up our hearts in glad - ness, As we now gath-

dos al pan de vi - da, Que_es fuen-te de glo - ria_e - ter -
er, one faith pro -fess - ing. Our life-giv - ing Bread, the Source

na, De for - ta - le - za y de_a - le - grí - a.
of our fu - ture Glo - ry, brings strength and bless - ing.

Estrofas / Verses

1. A ti_a - cu - di - mos se - dien - tos: ¡Ven, Se -
2. Per - do - na nues - tros pe - ca - dos: ¡Ven, Se -
3. Que no_ha - ya lu - chas fra - ter - nas: ¡Ven, Se -
1. We thirst for life - giv - ing wa - ter: Come, O
2. For - give our sins and our fail - ings: Come, O
3. Cast out all war and di - vi - sion: Come, O

ñor! Te - ne - mos fe_en tu mis - te - rio: ¡Ven, Se -
ñor! Por e - so_en ti con - fi - a - mos: ¡Ven, Se -
ñor! Ni_es -cla - vi - tud, ni mi - se - rias: ¡Ven, Se -
Lord. We know that you are now with us: Come, O
Lord. Re - mem - ber us in your mer - cy: Come, O
Lord. As well as sla - v'ry and mi - s'ry: Come, O

ñor!	Que	-	re	-	mos dar	-	te	la	vi	-	da:
ñor!	Y		ha	-	lla - re	-	mos	las	fuer	-	zas:
ñor!	A	-	par	-	ta_el o	-	dio	del	mun	-	do:
Lord.	*We*		*bring*		*our - selves*	*as*		*an*	*of*	-	*f'ring:*
Lord.	*The*		*strength*		*we*	*need*	*we*		*will*	*find*	*here:*
Lord.	*Through - out*			*the*	*world*	*ban*	-	*ish*	*ha*	-	*tred:*

¡Ven,	Se	-	ñor!	Con	sus	do - lo	-	res	y
¡Ven,	Se	-	ñor!	Pa	- ra_ol	- vi - dar		las	o -
¡Ven,	Se	-	ñor!	Que_e	- xis	- ta_un or	-	den	más
Come,	*O*		*Lord;*	*With*	*all*	*our joys*	*and*		*our*
Come,	*O*		*Lord,*	*To*	*bring*	*for - give - ness*			*to*
Come,	*O*		*Lord.*	*May*	*jus*	*- tice flou - rish*			*for*

D.C.

di	-	chas:	¡Ven,	Se	-	ñor!
fen	-	sas:	¡Ven,	Se	-	ñor!
jus	-	to:	¡Ven,	Se	-	ñor!
sor	-	*rows:*	*Come,*	*O*		*Lord.*
oth	-	*ers:*	*Come,*	*O*		*Lord.*
ev	-	*er:*	*Come,*	*O*		*Lord.*

Texto: Tradicional; tr. por Ronald F. Krisman, n.1946, © 2005, GIA Publications, Inc.
Música: Tradicional; arm. por Ronald F. Krisman, n.1946, © 2005, GIA Publications, Inc.

77 Song of the Body of Christ
Canción del Cuerpo de Cristo

Refrain / Estribillo

We come to share our sto - ry, we
Hoy ve - ni - mos a con - tar nues-tra_his - to - ria, com - par -

come to break the bread, We
tien - do_el pan ce - les - tial. Hoy ve -

Last time

come to know our ris - ing from the dead.
ni - mos jun - tos a ce - le - brar tu mis - te - rio pas - cual.

Last time

Verses

1. We come as your peo - ple, we
2. We are called to heal the bro - ken, to be
3. Bread of life and cup of prom - ise, in this
4. You will lead and we shall fol - low, you will
5. We will live and sing: "A - lo - ha," "Al - le -
   (live and sing your prais - es,)

come as your own, u - nit - ed with each
hope for the poor, we are called to feed the
meal we all are one. In our dy - ing and our
be the breath of life; liv - ing wa - ter, we are
lu - ia" is our song. May we live in love and

D.C.

oth - er, love finds a home.
hun - gry at our door.
ris - ing, may your king-dom come.
thirst - ing for your light.
peace our whole life long.

Estrofas

1. Hoy ve - ni - mos por - que so - mos tu pue - blo, re - na -
2. A sa - nar al en - fer - mo nos lla - mas, al an -
3. Pan de vi - da y san-gre de la a - lian - za, haz - nos
4. Nos guia - rás y te se - gui - re - mos. Nues-tro a -
5. Vi - vi - re - mos can - tan - do "A - lo - ja." "A - le -

ci - dos por tu per - dón, re - u - ni - dos en
sio - so, tu es - pe - ran - za tra - er, y al ham - brien - to, nues-
u - no en es - ta co - mu - nión. Que tu rei - no ven -
lien - to vi - tal tú se - rás. Nues-tra luz, en el dí - a
lu - ya" es nues - tra can - ción. Que vi - va - mos por siem-

D.C.

tu a - mor, y de un co - ra - zón.
tro a-li - men - to o - fre - cer.
ga en nues - tra trans - for-ma - ción.
y en la no - che bri - lla - rás.
pre en paz y fra - ter - na u - nión.

Text: David Haas, b.1957; tr. by Donna Peña, b.1955, and Ronald F. Krisman, b.1946
Tune: NO KE ANO' AHI AHI, Irregular, Hawaiian traditional, arr. by David Haas, b.1957
© 1989, 2004, GIA Publications, Inc.

78 Taste and See / Gusten y Vean

Refrain / Estribillo

Taste and see, taste and see the good - ness
Gus -ten y ve -an, gus-ten y ve-an qué bue - no_es

of the Lord. O taste and see,
el Se - ñor. Oh, gus -ten y ve-an,

taste and see the good - ness of the Lord,
gus-ten y ve -an qué bue - no_es el Se - ñor,

To verses / Last time

of the Lord. Lord.
el Se - ñor. ñor.

Verses

1. I will bless the Lord at all times.
2. Glo - ri - fy the Lord with me.
3. Wor - ship the Lord, all you peo - ple.

To -

Praise shall al-ways be on my lips;
geth-er let us all praise God's name.
You'll want for noth-ing if you ask.
my
I

soul shall glo-ry in the Lord for
called the Lord who an-swered me; from
Taste and see that the Lord is good; in

God has been so good to me.
all my trou-bles I was set free.
God we need put all our trust.

Estrofa 1

1. Ben - di - go al Se - ñor en to-do mo -men-to. Su a-la-

ban - za es-tá siem-pre en mi bo - ca. Mi

al - ma se glo - rí-a en el Se - ñor: los hu -

mil - des se a - le - gran al es - cu - char - lo.

Estrofa 2

2. La gran-de-za del Se-ñor pro-cla-men con-mi-go, y jun-tos en-sal-ce-mos su san-to nom-bre. A-cu-dí al Se-ñor, y_él me res-pon-dió: de to-dos mis te-mo-res me li-bró.

D.C.

Estrofa 3

3. Al Se-ñor a-do-ren, to-dos los pue-blos. Los que bus-can al Se-ñor no ca-re-cen de na-da. Gus-ten y ve-an su bon-dad; di-cho-sos los que se_a-co-gen a él.

D.C.

Text: Psalm 34; James E. Moore, Jr., b.1951; tr. by Ronald F. Krisman, b.1946
Tune: James E. Moore, Jr., b.1951
© 1983, 2005, GIA Publications, Inc.

Somos Pueblo Que Camina 79
Welcome, Pilgrims on the Journey

1. So - mos pue - blo que ca - mi - na
2. Los hu - mil - des y los po - bres
3. Es - te pan que Dios nos brin - da
1. Wel -come, pil - grims on the jour - ney,
2. To God's ta - ble are in - vit - ed
3. God will nour - ish our com - mun - ion

Por las sen - das del do - lor.
In - vi - ta - dos son de Dios.
A - li - men - ta nues - tra_u - nión.
Of - ten wea - ry and in pain.
All the low - ly and the poor.
With the fin - est heav'n - ly Bread.

A - cu - da-mos ju - bi - lo-sos a la ce - na del Se - ñor.
Join to-geth-er now, re - joic-ing at the ban - quet of the Lord.

4. Cristo_aquí se_hace presente,   *4. Christ has promised to be with us*
   Al reunirnos en su_amor.   *When we gather in his name.*

5. Los sedientos de justicia   *5. All who are athirst for justice,*
   Buscan su liberación.   *Hear God's liberating word.*

Texto: Manuel Dávila; tr. por Ronald F. Krisman, n.1946, © 2005, GIA Publications, Inc.
Música: Manuel Dávila, *Misa Popular Nicaragüense;* arm. por Ronald F. Krisman, n.1946, © 2005, GIA Publications, Inc.

80   Bread of Life from Heaven / Pan de Vida Eterna

Refrain / Estribillo

Bread of life from heav-en, your blood and bod - y
Pan de vi - da_e - ter - na, nos das tu cuer - po_y

we eat this
Has - ta que

giv - en, we eat this bread and drink this cup un-
san - gre. Has - ta que vuel - vas tú, Se - ñor, co-

Last time

til you come a - gain.
me - mos en tu_a - mor.

Last time

Verses / Estrofas

1. Break now the bread of Christ's sac - ri - fice; Giv - ing
2. Seek not the food that will pass a - way; Set your
3. Love as the One who, in love for you, Gave him -
4. Take in the light that will nev - er dim, Taste the
5. Dwell in the One who now dwells in you; Make your
6. Drink of this cup and de - clare his death; Eat this
7. Ven y com-par - te_el di - vi - no pan; De - mos
8. Es - te mis - te - rio_es el máx - i - mo sa - cri -
9. Ven a la me - sa de com - pa -sión, re - cor -
10. Hoy que co - me - mos del pan de_a -mor so - mos
11. Ce - na que nos re - pre - sen - ta hoy la vi - da,

thanks, hun - gry ones gath - er 'round. Eat all of you, and be
hearts on the food that en - dures. Come, learn the true and the
self for the life of the world. Come to the One who is
life that is strong - er than death. Live in the One who will
home in the life - giv - ing Word. Know on - ly Christ, Ho - ly
bread and be - lieve Eas - ter morn; Trust his re - turn and, with
gra - cias con gran co - ra - zón. Cris - to_es sus - ten - to que
fi - cio de fe y de_a - mor. Pan que nos lla - ma_a con-
de - mos a Cris - to Je - sús. Él nos da vi - da con
u - no en Cris - to Je - sús. Ce - na que_es fuen - te de_in-
muer - te y re - su -rrec - ción de Je - su - cris - to que_es

D.S.

sat - is - fied; in Christ's pres - ence the loaves will a - bound.
liv - ing way, that the full - ness of life may be yours.
food for you, that your hun - ger and thirst be no more.
come and then raise you up at the last with the blest.
One of God, and be - lieve in the truth you have heard.
ev - 'ry breath, praise the One in whom you are re - born.
u - ni - rá a los miem - bros de ca - da na - ción.
me - mo - rar y_a se - guir a Je - sús Sal - va - dor.
ple - ni - tud; Nos pro - te - ge_y nos guí - a_en su luz.
spi - ra - ción pa - ra ser en el mun - do la luz.
nues - tro Dios quien nos lla - ma_y nos da sal - va - ción.

Text: Based on John 6; adapt. by Susan R. Briehl, b.1952; tr. by Jaime Cortez, b.1963
Tune: Argentine folk melody; adapt. and verses by Marty Haugen, b.1950
© 2001, GIA Publications, Inc.

81 I Am the Bread of Life / Yo Soy el Pan de Vida

Verses / Estrofas

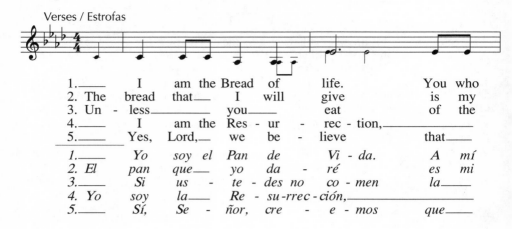

1.___ I am the Bread of life. You who
2. The bread that___ I will give is my
3. Un - less___ you___ eat of the
4.___ I am the Res - ur - rec - tion,___
5.___ Yes, Lord,___ we be - lieve that___

1.___ Yo soy el Pan de Vi - da. A mí
2. El pan que___ yo da - ré es mi
3.___ Si us - te - des no co - men la___
4. Yo soy la___ Re - su-rrec-ción,___
5.___ Sí, Se - ñor, cre - e - mos que___

come to me shall not hun - ger;___ and who be -
flesh for the life of the world,___ and if you
flesh of the Son of Man___ and___
I___ am the life.___ If you be -
you___ are the Christ,___ the___

ven - gan:___ no ten-drán ham - bre.___ En mí
car - ne, la vi - da del mun - do.___ Los que
car - ne del Hi - jo del Hom - bre,___ y no
Yo___ soy la Vi - da.___ Si en
tú_e - res___ el Me - sí - as,___ el___

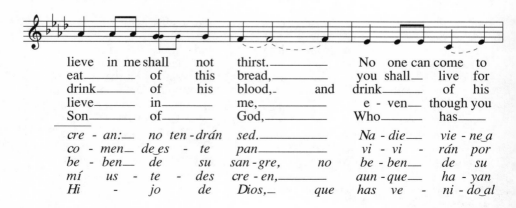

lieve in me shall not thirst.___ No one can come to
eat___ of this bread,___ you shall___ live for
drink___ of his blood,- and drink___ of his
lieve___ in___ me,___ e - ven___ though you
Son___ of___ God,___ Who___ has___

cre - an:___ no ten-drán sed.___ Na - die___ vie - ne_a
co - men de_es - te pan___ vi - vi - rán por
be - ben___ de su san - gre, no be - ben___ de su
mí us - te - des cre - en,___ aun - que___ ha - yan
Hi - jo de Dios,- que has ve - ni - do_al

me un - less the Fa - ther beck - ons.
ev - er,_____ you shall live for ev - er.
blood, you shall not have life with - in you.
die,_____ you shall live for ev - er.
come in - to_____ the_____ world._____
mí si mi Pa - dre no lo a - tra - e.
siem - pre,_____ vi - vi - rán por siem - pre.
san - gre, no po - drán te - ner mi vi - da.
muer - to,_____ vi - vi - rán por siem - pre.
mun - do_____ pa - ra re - di - mir - nos.

Refrain / Estribillo

And I will raise you up, and I will
Yo los re - su - ci - ta - ré, Yo los re -

raise you up, and I will raise you
su - ci - ta - ré, Yo los re - su - ci - ta -

up on the last day.
ré en el dí - a fi - nal.

Text: John 6 and 11; Suzanne Toolan, RSM, b.1927; tr. by anon., rev. by Ronald F. Krisman, b.1946
Tune: BREAD OF LIFE, Irregular with refrain; Suzanne Toolan, RSM, b.1927
© 1966, 1970, 1986, 1993, 2005, GIA Publications, Inc.

82 Corre el Viento
Wind and Cold Roar through the City Street

Estrofas / Verses

1. Co - rre el vien-to en es - ta gran ciu - dad, Mu - chos tem - bla-
2. Es - ta gran ciu - dad pro - gre - sa - rá, Mu - chos su - fri-
3. Gue - rras y más gue - rras por la paz, Mu - chos mo - ri-

1. Wind and cold roar through the cit - y street; Some folk have no
2. Those with - in may swell with civ - ic pride; Man - y wait out-
3. Vi - o - lence and ha - tred, near and far, Ter - ror, slaugh - ter,

rán: Per - dón, Se - ñor. Pa - ra u - nos hoy ha - brá ca-
rán: Per - dón, Se - ñor. Pa - ra u - nos, la o - por - tu - ni-
rán: Per - dón, Se - ñor. Mu - chas ma - nos se le - van - ta-

heat: For -give us, Lord. Man - y have warm homes, wool clothes to
side: For -give us, Lord. Some have man - y chanc - es to suc-
war: For -give us, Lord. You in - sist the hun - gry shall be

lor; Pa - ra o - tros, no; Per - dón, Se - ñor.
dad; Pa - ra o - tros, no; Per - dón, Se - ñor.
rán Re - cla-man - do pan: Per - dón, Se - ñor.

wear; This is so un - fair: For - give us, Lord.
ceed; Oth -ers live in need: For - give us, Lord.
fed; Let us give them bread: For - give us, Lord.

Estribillo / Refrain

A - yú - da-nos a en-ten - der Nues - tra cul - pa,
Help us grasp how this is our sin; Teach us, save us

oh Se - ñor. Nues-tras a - le - grí - as son do-
by your Cross, For the things we crave and seek to

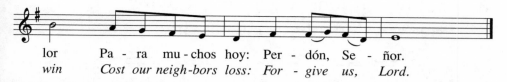

lor   Pa - ra   mu - chos   hoy: Per - dón,   Se - ñor.
win   Cost our neigh-bors loss: For - give   us,   Lord.

Texto: Homero R. Perera, © 1978; tr. por Madeleine Forell Marshall, n.1946, © 2003, Augsburg Fortress
Música: PERDON, SEÑOR, 9 9 9 9 con estribillo; Homero R. Perera, © 1978; arm. por Ronald F. Krisman, n.1946, © 2005, GIA Publications, Inc.

83 Softly and Tenderly Jesus Is Calling
Tierno y Amante, Jesús Nos Invita

1. Soft - ly and ten - der - ly Je - sus is call - ing,
2. Why should we tar - ry when Je - sus is plead - ing,
3. Time is now fleet - ing, the mo - ments are pass - ing,
4. O for the won - der - ful love He has prom - ised,

1. *Tier - no y a - man - te, Je - sús nos in - vi - ta.*
2. *Si - gue lla - man - do; ¿por qué di - la - ta - mos?*
3. *El tiem - po vue - la, lo - grar - lo con - vie - ne,*
4. *¡Oh ma - ra - vi - lla de a - mor pro - me - ti - do*

Call - ing for you and for me; See, on the por - tals He's
Plead - ing for you and for me? Why should we lin - ger and
Pass - ing from you and from me; Shad - ows are gath - er - ing,
Prom - ised for you and for me; Though we have sinned He has

Llá - ma - te a ti, y a mí. Mí - ra - le a - llá en la
Llá - ma - te a ti, y a mí. Tan - tas mer - ce - des en
Cris - to te lla - ma a ti. Vie - nen las som - bras y
Tan - to a ti co - mo a mí! Ven y re - ci - be el per -

wait - ing and watch - ing, Watch - ing for you and for me.
heed not His mer - cies, Mer - cies for you and for me?
death - beds are com - ing, Com - ing for you and for me.
mer - cy and par - don, Par - don for you and for me.

puer - ta es - pe - ran - do; A - guar - da a ti y a mí.
po - co ten - dre - mos. Á - ma - te a ti y a mí.
vie - ne la muer - te, Vie - nen por ti y por mí.
dón o - fre - ci - do, Da - do de gra - cia a ti.

Come home, come home,
¡Ve - nid, ve - nid,

Come home, come home,
¡Ve - nid, ve - nid,

Come home, come home,
¡Ve - nid, ve - nid,

Come home,
¡Ve - nid,

Ye who are wea-ry, come home; Ear-nest-ly, ten-der-ly,
Tris-tes, can-sa-dos, ve - nid! Tier - no y_a-man-te, Je -

Je - sus is call-ing— Call-ing, "O sin-ner, come home!"
sús nos in - vi - ta: ¡Oh pe - ca - do-res, ve - nid!

Text: Will L. Thompson, 1847-1909; vss. 1, 2, 4, tr. by E. L. Maxwell; vs. 3 tr. by Pedro Grado, 1862-1923, adapt. by H. C. Ball
Tune: THOMPSON, 11 7 11 7 with refrain; Will L. Thompson, 1847-1909

84 O Sanctissima / O Most Virtuous
Oh Santísima

1. O sanctíssima, O piíssima,
2. Tu solátium Et refúgium,
3. Ecce débiles, Per quam flébiles,

1. *O most virtuous And most pious,*
2. *Our protection and Consolation,*
3. *See us powerless In our hopelessness:*

1. ¡Oh Santísima, Oh purísima,
2. ¡Clementísima, Fidelísima,
3. ¡Prudentísima, Y fortísima,

Dulcis virgo María!
Virgo mater María!
Salva nos, O María!

Dearest maiden, sweet Mary,
Virgin mother, good Mary,
Aid us, save us, O Mary!

Dulce Virgen María!
Virgen, Madre María!
Sálvanos, oh María!

Mater amáta, In temeráta,
Quidquid optámus, Per te sperámus,
Tolle languóres, Sana dolóres,

Mother affectionate, Virgin inviolate,
What-e'er our souls desire, May you help us to acquire.
Wipe away the tears we shed, Heal us of our grief and dread.

¡Madre amada! ¡Inmaculada!
Todo, si pides, Tú nos consiques,
¡Haznos seguros, Castos y puros!

O	-	ra,	o	-	ra pro	no	bis.
O	-	ra,	o	-	ra pro	no	bis.
O	-	ra,	o	-	ra pro	no	bis.
In	- ter - cede	and	pray	for	us,	O	Mar - y!
In	- ter - cede	and	pray	for	us,	O	Mar - y!
In	- ter - cede	and	pray	for	us,	O	Mar - y!
¡Rue	- ga,	rue - ga	por	no	- so	- tros!
¡Rue	- ga,	rue - ga	por	no	- so	- tros!
¡Rue	- ga,	rue - ga	por	no	- so	- tros!

4. Virgo, réspice,
Mater, ádspice,
Audi nos, María!
Tu medicínam,
Portas divínam;
Ora, ora pro nobis.

4. *Maiden, look on us,*
Mother, care for us.
Hear our pleas, O Mary!
Balm and our surety,
Gateway to divinity,
Intercede and pray for us,
O Mary!

4. *¡Invictísima,*
Piadosísima,
Pídenos, oh María!
Muerte dichosa,
Vida gloriosa!
¡Ruega, ruega por
nosotros!

Text: St. 1, *Stimmen der Völker in Liedern*, 1807; st. 2, *Arundel Hymnal*, 1902; English tr. by Neil Borgstrom, b.1953, © 1994, GIA Publications, Inc.;
    Spanish tr., traditional
Tune: O DU FRÖLICHE, 55 7 55 7; Tattersall's *Improved Psalmody*, 1794

85 Como Estrella en Claro Cielo
As a Star on Cloudless Evenings

1. Co - mo_es - tre - lla_en cla - ro cie - lo De ful - gen - te res - plan - dor, Es - co - gi - da fue Ma - rí - a Por de - sig - nio del Se - ñor.
2. Fue un án - gel quien le die - ra Be - llas nue - vas de sa - lud, Y_a me - dia - dos de_u - na no - che Dios al mun - do_en - vió la luz.
3. De la pa - ja al ma - de - ro Fue_a su hi - jo siem - pre fiel Y_en - tre lá - gri - mas y ri - sas Con - sa - gró su vi - da_a Él.
4. Glo - ria_al Pa - dre y al Hi - jo, Y_al Es - pí - ri - tu_en ver - dad, Co - mo e - ra al prin - ci - pio, Es a - ho - ra y se - rá.

1. As a star on cloud-less eve - nings Will with great - er bril - liance shine, So re - splen -dent was the maid - en Cho - sen for the Lord's de - sign:
2. When the an - gel spoke to Mar - y, His good news brought great de - light: It was God's on - ly - be - got - ten, The Cre -
3. From the sta - ble to the hill - side Mar - y's faith would nev - er dim: In her tears and in her laugh - ter She had pledged her life to Him. As we cel - e - brate her glad - ness, We re -
4. To the Fa - ther, Son, and Spir - it, Glo - ry, hon - or, thanks, and praise, As it was in the be - gin - ning And shall be for end - less days. Let our prayers rise up like in - cense To the

Fair -est rose in all earth's gar - den, Bloom -ing

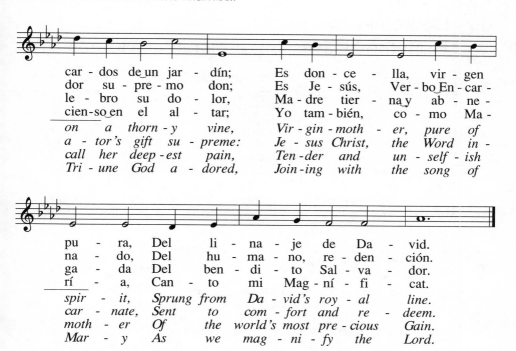

car - dos de un jar - dín;   Es don - ce - lla, vir - gen
dor su - pre - mo don;   Es Je - sús, Ver - bo En - car -
le - bro su do - lor,   Ma - dre tier - na y ab - ne -
cien-so en el al - tar;   Yo tam - bién, co - mo Ma -
on   a thorn - y vine,   *Vir - gin - moth - er, pure of*
a - tor's gift su - preme: *Je - sus Christ, the Word in -*
call her deep - est pain, *Ten - der and un - self - ish*
Tri - une God a - dored,   *Join -ing with the song of*

pu - ra, Del li - na - je de Da - vid.
na - do, Del hu - ma - no, re - den - ción.
ga - da Del ben - di - to Sal - va - dor.
rí - a, Can - to mi Mag - ní - fi - cat.
spir - it, Sprung from Da - vid's roy - al line.
car - nate, Sent to com - fort and re - deem.
moth - er Of the world's most pre - cious Gain.
Mar - y As we mag - ni - fy the Lord.

Texto: Skinner Chávez-Melo, 1944-1992, © 1987, Juan Francisco Chávez; tr. por Ronald F. Krisman, b.1946, © 2005, GIA Publications, Inc.
Música: RAQUEL, 8 7 8 7 D; Skinner Chávez-Melo, 1944-1992, © 1987, Juan Francisco Chávez

86 Desde el Cielo
From the Heavens on a Beautiful Morning

Estribillo Des - de el cie - lo u - na her - mo - sa ma - ña - na,
1. Su lle - ga - da lle - nó de a - le - grí - a,
2. Su - pli - can - te jun - ta - ba las ma - nos,
3. Jun - to al mon - te pa - sa - ba Juan Die - go,

Refrain From the heav'ns on a beau - ti - ful morn - ing,
1. Her ar - ri - val brought joy o - ver - flow - ing,
2. She was clasp - ing her hands, soft - ly pray - ing,
3. From the hill - side Juan Die - go was round - ing,

Des - de el cie - lo u - na her - mo - sa ma - ña - na,
Su lle - ga - da lle - nó de a - le - grí - a,
Su - pli - can - te jun - ta - ba las ma - nos.
Jun - to al mon - te pa - sa - ba Juan Die - go.
From the heav'ns on a beau - ti - ful morn - ing,
Her ar - ri - val brought joy o - ver - flow - ing,
She was clasp - ing her hands, soft - ly pray - ing,
From the hill - side Juan Die - go was round - ing,

La Gua - da - lu - pa - na, la Gua - da - lu - pa - na,
De paz y ar - mo - ní - a, de paz y ar - mo - ní - a,
Y e - ran me - xi - ca - nos, y e - ran me - xi - ca - nos,
Y a - cer - có - se lue - go, y a - cer - có - se lue - go,
Ra - diant light was pour - ing, ra - diant light was pour - ing,
Peace and con - cord grow - ing, peace and con - cord grow - ing,
Face and pos - ture say - ing, face and pos - ture say - ing,
Mu - sic sweet - ly sound - ing, mu - sic sweet - ly sound - ing,

La Gua - da - lu - pa - na ba - jó al Te - pe - yac.
De paz y ar - mo - ní - a to - do el A - ná - huac.
Y e - ran me - xi - ca - nos su por - te y su faz.
Y a - cer - có - se lue - go al o - ír can - tar.
La Gua - da - lu - pa - na came to Te - pe - yac.
Peace and con - cord grow - ing in the A - ná - huac.
She was Me - xi - ca - na, like the peo - ple there.
Mu - sic sweet - ly sound - ing filled the cool, crisp air.

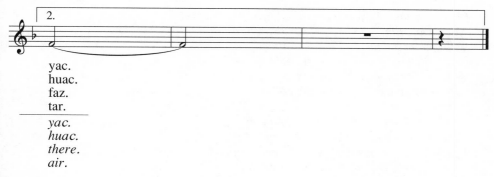

yac.
huac.
faz.
tar.

yac.
huac.
there.
air.

4. "Juan Dieguito," la Virgen le dijo,
   "Juan Dieguito," la Virgen le dijo,
   "Este cerro_elijo, este cerro_elijo,
   Este cerro_elijo para_hacer mi_altar."
   "Este cerro_elijo, este cerro_elijo,
   Este cerro_elijo para_hacer mi_altar."

5. Y_en la tilma_entre rosas pintadas,
   Y_en la tilma_entre rosas pintadas,
   Su_imagen amada, su_imagen amada,
   Su_imagen amada se dignó dejar.
   Su_imagen amada, su_imagen amada,
   Su_imagen amada se dignó dejar.

6. Desde_entonces para_el Mexicano,
   Desde_entonces para la Mexicana,
   Ser Guadalupano, ser Guadalupana,
   Ser Guadalupanos es algo_esencial.
   Ser Guadalupano, ser Guadalupana,
   Ser Guadalupanos es algo_esencial.

7. Madrecita de los Mexicanos,*
   Madrecita de los Mexicanos,
   Que_estás en el cielo, que_estás en el cielo,
   Que_estás en el cielo, ruega_a Dios por nos.
   Que_estás en el cielo, que_estás en el cielo,
   Que_estás en el cielo, ruega_a Dios por nos.

8. En sus penas se postra de_hinojos,
   En sus penas se postra de_hinojos,
   Y_eleva sus ojos, y_eleva sus ojos,
   Y_eleva sus ojos hacia_el Tepeyac.
   Y_eleva sus ojos, y_eleva sus ojos,
   Y_eleva sus ojos hacia_el Tepeyac.

Texto alternativo / alternate text: Madrecita de todos nosotros (2 x)

4. *"Juan Dieguito," the Virgin called gently.*
   "Juan Dieguito," the Virgin called gently.
   Telling him intently, telling him intently,
   "This hill I have chosen for my holy shrine."
   Telling him intently, telling him intently,
   "This hill I have chosen for my holy shrine."

5. *Roses fell from his cloak, brightly tinted,*
   Roses fell from his cloak, brightly tinted,
   Leaving there imprinted, leaving there imprinted,
   Leaving there the image of the Virgin fair.
   Leaving there imprinted, leaving there imprinted
   Leaving there the image of the Virgin fair.

6. *From that time forward, each Mexicano,*
   From that time forward, each Mexicana,
   True Guadalupano, true Guadalupana,
   True Guadalupanos all are born to be.
   True Guadalupano, true Guadalupana,
   True Guadalupanos all are born to be.

7. *Madrecita to all peoples given,*
   Madrecita to all peoples given,
   As the Queen of Heaven, as the Queen of Heaven,
   As the Queen of Heaven, kindly pray for us.
   As the Queen of Heaven, as the Queen of Heaven,
   As the Queen of Heaven, kindly pray for us.

8. *We approach you in love, humbly kneeling,*
   We approach you in love, humbly kneeling,
   Earnestly appealing, earnestly appealing,
   Lifting up our eyes and hearts to Tepeyac.
   Earnestly appealing, earnestly appealing,
   Lifting up our eyes and hearts to Tepeyac.

Texto: Tradicional; tr. por Mary Louise Bringle, n.1953, © 2005, GIA Publications, Inc.
Música: Tradicional; arm. por Ronald F. Krisman, n.1946, © 2005, GIA Publications, Inc.

Reconocimientos / Acknowledgments 87

All music found from nos. 1 to 25 is copyright by GIA Publications, Inc. Please refer to nos. 1 to 25 for specific copyright dates.

26 Spanish tr.: vss. 1, 4, 5, © 1964, Publicaciones *El Escudo;* vss. 2, 7, © 1962, Federico J. Pagura; vss. 3, 6, © Editorial Avance Luterano Acc.: © 1975, GIA Publications, Inc.
27 Traducción y arm.: © 2005, GIA Publications, Inc.
28 © 1982, 2005, GIA Publications, Inc.
29 Spanish tr.: © 2005, GIA Publications, Inc. Harm.: © 1958, The Basilian Fathers, assigned to Ralph Jusko Publications, Inc.
30 Traducción y arm.: © 2005, GIA Publications, Inc.
32 Spanish Text: © 1996, Abingdon Press (Admin. by THE COPYRIGHT COMPANY, Nashville, TN) Harm.: © 1989, The United Methodist Publishing House (Admin. by THE COPYRIGHT COMPANY, Nashville, TN) All Rights Reserved. International Copyright Secured. Used By Permission.
35 Text: © 1994 and tr., © 1996, Hope Publishing Company, Carol Stream, IL 60188. All rights reserved. Used by permission. Tune: © 2003, GIA Publications, Inc.
36 Text adapt.: © Mrs. John W. Work, III; trans., © Anita González. Harm.: © 1995, GIA Publications, Inc.
38 Traducción y arm.: © 2005, GIA Publications, Inc.
39 © 1990, 1991, 2005, GIA Publications, Inc.
40 Traducción: © 1992, Pilgrim Press. Todos los derechos reservados. Música: © 1988, Pablo D. Sosa
41 © 1981, 2005, Les Presses de Taizé, GIA Publications, Inc., agent
42 © 1997, 2005, GIA Publications, Inc.
43 Text and music: © 1974 Hope Publishing Co. Spanish tr.: © Hope Publishing Co., Carol Stream, IL 60188. All rights reserved. Used by permission.
44 Traducción y arm.: © 2005, GIA Publications, Inc.
45 Text and tune: © 1969, and arr., © 1982, Hope Publishing Co. Spanish tr.: © Hope Publishing Co., Carol Stream, IL 60188. All rights reserved. Used by permission.

46 Traducción y arm.: 2005, GIA Publications, Inc.
47 Text: Vss. 1, 2, 4, 5, © Federico J. Pagura; vs. 3, © 1970, Lois Kroehler. Harm.: © 1987, GIA Publications, Inc.
48 Text (English and Spanish) and tune: © 1973, Word of God Music. (Admin. by THE COPYRIGHT COMPANY, Nashville, TN) All rights reserved. International Copyright Secured. Used by permission.
49 © 1986, 2005, GIA Publications, Inc.
50 Traducción y arm.: © 2005, GIA Publications, Inc.
51 Spanish tr.: © 1962, Federico J. Pagura. Acc.: © 1975, GIA Publications, Inc.
52 Text and tune: © 1976, Fred Bock Music Co. Spanish tr.: © 1987, Barbara Mink
53 Texto: © 1979, Editorial Bonum. Traducción: © 1993, Pilgrim Press. Todos los derechos reservados. Arm.: © 1991, Editorial Concordia
54 © 1981, 1982, 1987, 2005, GIA Publications, Inc.
55 Traducción y arm.: © 2005, GIA Publications, Inc.
56 Text: © 1988, Oxford University Press. Used by permission. All rights reserved. Harm.: © The Trustees of Downside Abbey, Bath BA3 4RH, UK
58 Traducción y arm.: © 2005, GIA Publications, Inc.
59 Traducción y arm.: © 2005, GIA Publications, Inc.
60 Text and tune: © 1980, Savgos Music, Inc. Administered by Malaco Music Group. P.O. Box 9287, Jackson, MS 39206. Spanish tr.: © 2005, GIA Publications, Inc.
61 Traducción: © 1998, Augsburg Fortress. Usado con permiso.
62 English text: © David Higham Assoc. Ltd. Spanish tr.: © 1987, Comisión de "Albricias." Used with permission. Acc: © 1999, GIA Publications, Inc.
63 © 1966, F.E.L. Publications, assigned to The Lorenz Corp., 1991. All rights reserved. Reproduced by permission of The Lorenz Corp., Dayton, OH.
64 © 1985, 2005, GIA Publications, Inc.

Acknowledgments / Reconocimientos

Índice de Títulos y de Primeras Líneas

Index of First Lines and Common Titles